Gunning for the Red Baron

Number Seven:

C. A. Brannen Series

Gunning

Texas A&M University Press
College Station

for the Red Baron

LEON BENNETT

ISBN 1-58544-507-X

Contents

Acknowledgments

Special thanks are owed the plucky workers of the Public Record Office (Kew, London) and the RAF Museum (Hendon, London), who tolerated my demands—those of a non-tax-paying foreigner. Without these magnificent British sources, the book would lack content.

My wife Rachelle, fortunately trained to decipher military code, proved able to break down software procedures and airline schedules as well. With gusto, she guided my faltering steps through the writing process. Without her there would be no manuscript.

Discussions with my brother Stewart, physicist (Ph.D.) and optics expert, have centered on the reality of gunnery optical illusions. Without his knowledgeable endorsement, I would hesitate to put forth so sweeping a rationale for tracer disappointments.

Finally, hats off to the Red Baron. In a war of millions, he proved that individuals still counted, and that skill plus bravery could beat probability. As we each go about life in our own mad world, it's a lesson worth pondering.

Gunning for the Red Baron

Introduction

WHY AN AIR SERVICE IN AN INFANTRY WAR? Why bother with air combat when the taking of ground was everything?

Experience showed certain aspects of flight to be immediately profitable. It paid to keep an eye on the enemy—his positions, movements, and supplies—and with wings it was possible to see miles beyond the front lines. The guidance of artillery fire made use of the same "eye in the sky" ability. No balloon could hope to compete. Winged observation became a highly successful form of ground support, used throughout the war.

With vision found to be important, denying its virtues to the other side came next. The task was to shoot down his observation aircraft. Aerial duels became useful for a practical reason: blinding the enemy.

However, vision capability alone seemed a disappointingly minor advantage. Much more had been expected from aircraft. What of victory through strategic bombing, or perhaps through the terrorization of the civilian population? They were not to be. By midwar it was clear—even to believers—that the early hopes of victory through air power were unrealistic. As all-out supporter Winston S. Churchill admitted in October 1917, air power couldn't "finish the war by itself." If anything, the reverse was true, for the result of bombing—Zeppelin and airplane—upon the British population had "seen the combative spirit of the people roused, and not quelled."[1]

What then could be done with wings to speed the end of the war? He had a plan. As a start, destroy the enemy's air forces. No matter what the price; no matter what other

The Price Paid

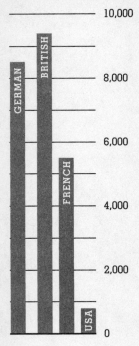

Air Service Casualties 1914–1918
Total Killed or Missing

Efficient German aircrew usage led to low losses as compared to the aggressive British, careful French, and late-appearing Americans. *Source:* original drawing. Chart data: USA, Cooke, *U.S. Air Service in the Great War*, 222; British and French, Jones, *War in the Air*, vol. 7, 160; German, Christienne and Lissarrague, *History of French Military Aviation*, 130.

tempting objective must be ignored. Once the enemy lacked an air force, he was incapable of resisting invasion— not *through* the front lines, but *over* them—bringing troops to essential bridges and rail lines, cutting off and isolating the enemy's frontline troops. Let the enemy's best wither while the real fight—ordinary infantry battle— took place fifty or more miles beyond the front lines. Unprepared and able to field only second-rate units of the local guard type, the enemy would soon be defeated. Battle would move toward Germany itself. The cycle would repeat. Unprotected skies would again permit the landing of additional troops and supplies. Inevitably, German surrender would result.

His plan required one given: destruction of the German Air Service. To Churchill this goal was so important that he was willing to sacrifice "2,000 to 3,000 airplanes, their pilots being killed or captured."[2] His very willingness to accept a loss of this magnitude was a measure of the plan's importance. (See Great War totals.)

Summing Churchill's concept: having one's Air Service defeated opened the possibility for defeat on the ground. Although little more than a series of conjectures, this possibility couldn't be ignored. His plan might have worked. In reality, it wasn't pursued. Instead it became the war's key rationale for aerial fighting prowess: by being strong in the air, a nation could prevent one form of disaster to its ground forces. Here was a most powerful, albeit negative, incentive: the side with aerial supremacy was much less likely to lose an infantry war.

Churchill's scheme was apparent to German strategists, as was the means of successful opposition: under no circumstances was the German Air Service to be crushed. Success in defeating enemy airplanes became an essential role of the Service. Responding to the new emphasis on aerial supremacy, Germany trained its fighter or pursuit pilots as specialists, abandoning its traditional general-purpose instruction.[3] Fighter pilots were to be a breed apart. What made for good ones? German Air Service Chief General Ernst von Hoeppner noted that some of the best started out as cavalry officers; for example, there was Manfred von Richthofen (the Red Baron). Wanted were more young cavalrymen—thousands more—and he pressed for transfers over the objections of furious cavalry generals.[4]

Oddly enough, the British agreed with the notion of cavalry as a superb breeding ground, believing that the "good hands" necessary in horsemanship described those very skills possessed by superior pilots. In other words, sensitivity to the quirks of beasts and machines was a single shared trait, and a most valuable one. Concerning importance, the French didn't agree. As they saw it, the key piloting attribute was coolness in action, as measured by a muted reaction to extreme stress. The Americans, new to the war and uncertain, sought only perfect physical specimens as pilots, reasoning that physical perfection implied possession of all the right traits. Sometimes this was the case—but only sometimes.

Men seek to measure whatever is important, and the notion of counting and assigning aerial victories started. Combat scores supplied a romantic aspect of war for those at home. With armies condemned to sit in trenches mired in mud and filth, aerial duels preserved a sense of war as it should be, with win or lose, do or die, written cleanly in the sky. Here was a means of personalizing the war with heroes and villains whose fortunes could be followed in the newspapers, rather like sports champions. France contributed the concept of the ace: a pilot or gunner who has destroyed five or more enemies. Favorites granted interviews and posed for picture postcards. The sports-mad British public pursued the career of enemy German ace Richthofen with tremendous enthusiasm and even managed to buy copies of his translated 1917 memoirs—the original German version having been sneaked in through neutral Sweden.

To the Air Services ace celebrity value was a major plus, boosting recruiting. In addition to bolstering morale, the aces had a deeper significance. Their undeniable skills and the dependence of national security upon those skills stood as reassuring proof—the individual still counted.

Just as important was the right airplane. Wanted was the best fighting machine. However, the nature of airplane design rarely leads to a solution that is tops in every department. Products found outstanding in one area are likely to be barely adequate in others. In aerial fighting, speed was important, but so was maneuverability. An advantage of speed meant the ability to enter or quit combat when desired. Superior maneuverability meant the ability to close with a murderous enemy in safety. How much speed was to be traded off to gain maneuverability? Not easy, that one, for any designer or any Air Service. Yet that issue had much to do with determining victory or defeat in combat. Opting for the right design compromise was as important as choosing the right kind of men.

The Rival Aircraft (ca. 1915)

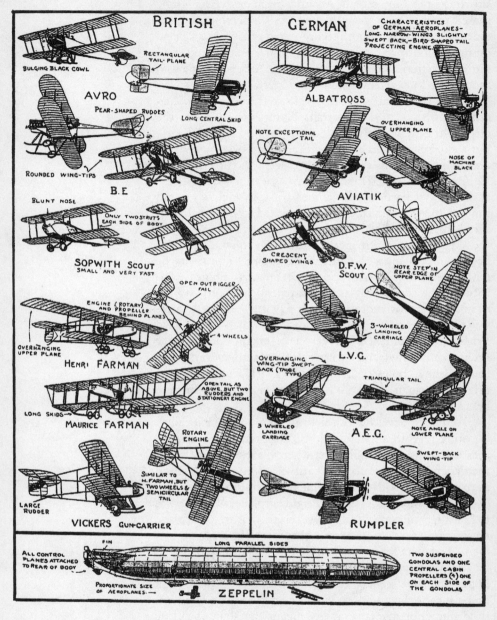

At war's start, Army aircraft were mostly gentle observation and cooperation types. True fighting aircraft were yet to come. *Source: The Aeroplane*, August 11, 1915, 157.

This book is concerned with the craft of shooting down airplanes in the Great War. At issue are men, weapons, airplanes, and tactics. Examined are the lessons learned as every Air Service fought for dominance. Answers came grudgingly, with even a natural like Richthofen puzzled by his inability to hit aerial targets when serving an early hitch as a gunner/observer.[5] His surprise was shared by many. Traditional hunting skills did little to assure air-shooting accuracy, and the curse of jammed guns had no civil counterpart. It was important not only to be of the right kind but also to have the right weapon rather than the obvious one—an elephant gun.

Even if supplied with the right weapon, the next step—aiming it—turned out to be far from easy. There was no time to do the traditional hunter's setting of gun sights. What then?

One possibility was guidance from tracers, designed to act as a bullet path "highliter." Yet tracers gave rise to a series of flaws and optical illusions acting to destroy whatever assistive value they might have had. We shall explore these, testing the reader's ability to see through the numerous catches.

The combat experience itself, with decisions depending on aircraft performance traits, is examined by means of a classic battle between Richthofen and Capt. Lanoe G. Hawker. Offered in blow-by-blow fashion, we watch as they circle and scheme, each hoping that the steadily decreasing altitude will act in his favor.

We end with the men: those who were high-scoring aces. What special quality motivated them? What of those who saw as insufficient the usual goal of forty victories and out? How many victories were possible? Using modern statistical projection schemes we arrive at what might have been: the Red Baron's projected score in a more reasonable world, along with some thoughts on his demise.

Let us start with a simpler issue, though a puzzle in 1912. Was it really possible to shoot down an airplane? Moving at high speed and readily able to maneuver, all at high altitude, was it really vulnerable? Weren't bullets too little and too late?

1

Could It Be Done?

ELIMINATE AN AERIAL ENEMY? TO PREWAR dreamers, it was quite simple. Merely climb above your unsuspecting victim and give him a full clip from an automatic pistol, "if possible, Mauser Pistols."[1]

Some preparation was necessary; for accuracy and reloading purposes, "unless gloves are very thin, they must be easily removable." If your mount consisted of a tractor type airplane, the sort carrying its engine/propeller up front, care was necessary to avoid holing your own propeller or lower wing. In 1914, given good marksmanship, a brace of automatic pistols, a "chrome steel bucket seat" (should the enemy return fire), and an airplane performance equal or superior to your enemy, the outcome seemed almost certain to Royal Flying Corps hot bloods.[2]

It wasn't so. Actually, the plan was so much nonsense, a delicious fiction of the type that becomes stronger than truth. In this case, a curious definition for aerial victory supported the nonsense, that is: "the enemy was driven down." Reasonable enemies go away when aware that somebody is pegging shots at them. After all, they can always return. Should your side interpret a reasonable enemy's departure as a "driven down" victory, so be it. He will only shrug at your childish scoring system.

Imaginary British aerial victories grew until well into 1915. After a year of war, in August 1915, a skeptical Maj. Hugh Dowding, later to become a planner of Battle of Britain strategy, announced: "I can not find any pilots or observers who *know* that they have hit a hostile aeroplane."[3] In a quiet way, he was blowing a whistle. Perhaps it was possible to shoot down an enemy aircraft in principle,

An Unlikely Means

A British Bristol tackles a German Taube in a real-life incident over Flanders, November 1914. The attack failed—he missed. *Source: Flying,* November 1914, 293.

but the practical problems of accuracy were overwhelming. As he pointed out, merely inventing a superior gun sight wasn't the answer, for split-second combat encounters permitted no time to work a "scientific" sight.

What then was the answer? A larger question emerges: why did air-conscious nations enter the "air age" unprepared to fend off enemy airplanes? There was not a single prescient country; all were equally slack—how could this be?

Each nation regarded the onset of the air age as part boon, part threat. Much depended on the national psyche, and

Impresario and Intellectual

Mervyn O'Gorman, Supt. of the Royal Aircraft Factory and head of British Army aircraft development. *Source:* (top) *Flight,* December 28, 1912, 1210; (bottom) Courtesy Imperial War Museum.

even more on the state of the national coffers. To the United States, despite the Wright brothers, air travel appeared to offer little gain. A few small firms such as Curtiss could be supported to supply machines for aerial circuses and army reconnaissance, but that was all.

Germany was quick to see the airship, and especially the rigid airship or zeppelin, as a practical and profitable means of travel throughout Central Europe. As for airplanes, the breed was cursed with a limited range and light payload. At best, only a limited role was possible: here was a sportsman's toy and an eye for the army, but no more. To suggest airplane bombing or aerial fighting was so much Sunday Supplement nonsense.

The British moved uncertainly. Early airship enthusiasm faded as the high cost of development became clear. By 1912 only eight airship piloting licenses had been granted to Britons, and even those few pilots had little chance to practice their skill; there were many more pilots than airships.[4]

Mayfly, a single large British airship of the rigid type costing as much as fifty airplanes, had ended badly in 1911, hung up on a doorframe while exiting its hangar against a strong crosswind. The delicate airship structure was crushed; a total loss resulted. Lacking in even a single noteworthy flight to offset the resulting ridicule ("it May Fly or May Not"[5]), the British Navy's Winston Churchill moved gingerly on the subject of further airship commitments. It was better to fund private airplane manufacturers. Money was tight and the inevitable blunders surrounding pioneering development were more easily buried if the scale was small. Airplanes and tiny airships it would be—they were cheap.

British Army policy was made clear by the appointment of David Henderson as the effective head of the new Royal Flying Corps (RFC) (September 1913). Here was a degreed engineer and functioning intellectual who had quite literally written the book on reconnaissance, based on his Boer War experience.[6] His very choice made the premier mission of the RFC clear—reconnaissance. Whether any of the airplane's other war potentials—bombing and fighting—were to be realized would depend on the input of other men. First among these was Mervyn O'Gorman, appointed superintendent of the government's in-house source of R & D, the Royal Aircraft Factory.

If Henderson was an intellectual, O'Gorman was the intellectual's intellectual, a natural fit at any university but

Chapter 1

On the Job

seemingly out of place in an airplane factory environment. His striking intelligence was bolstered with an easy wit and a great deal of charm. He could solve differential equations on his own, a rare ability among CEOs then or now. He found it easy to apply advanced gyroscopic theory to the problem of rotary engines, turning out a research report that still has value.[7] He was even superb at certain practical problems: forged streamline wires were his own invention.[8] If there was a catch, it consisted of the usual intellectual's flaw: a tendency to reject any world construct at odds with his own; he had too great a respect for his own brain power. Then there was his outsized ambition: the wish to be the greatest aircraft impresario of them all. In early pre-war days these drawbacks were not obvious. Apparent was a most formidable talent, bolstered with an additional advantage: he got along well with Henderson.

In forming a new bureau, much is always left undefined. The general's gentlemanly lack of interest in meddling was a key factor in O'Gorman's rise. Although Henderson was free to reject O'Gorman's output, he accepted Royal Aircraft Factory products without complaint until well into the war. O'Gorman seemed highly competent, and if overly ambitious, Henderson could see no

O'Gorman (tallest civilian, right) judging the landing speed of a Maurice-Farman biplane at the 1912 Military Trials. Source: *The Aero*, September, 1912, 257.

Target Kite

harm in his energetic employee. In time O'Gorman's limitations would lead to much trauma. However, at the moment the Great War was far off and O'Gorman was concerned with a seemingly straight technical issue: could airplanes be shot down, yes or no?

For obvious reasons O'Gorman couldn't shoot down real aircraft, and so divided the problem into bite-sized portions—shooting at a moving kite from the ground, and separately, from an aircraft downward at a ground-mounted target. His experiments of 1912 strongly influenced the entire prewar British approach to gunnery and aircraft design.

The army turf at Shoeburyness was chosen for its remoteness and railroad line, offering an armored locomotive suited for pulling a large kite at a fair speed (20 MPH).[9] The target kite was a Pilot Type B, ordinarily used for stabilizing a still larger British Army man-carrying observation kite.

Type B consisted of a basic boxkite with airplanelike winglets attached at fore and aft locations. With a span in the 8- to 9-foot range depending on the dihedral adjustment, the kite proved stable and well able to accept bullet strikes. As for its limited size, Factory intellectuals came to accept 20 square feet as a warplane's critical area, containing a pilot, passenger, engine, fuel, and oil tanks.[10] The kite area would do as a representation of the critical portion.

Antiaircraft fire came from forty-eight riflemen carefully selected to offer an army-wide average of skill, with

Kite Shooting Layout

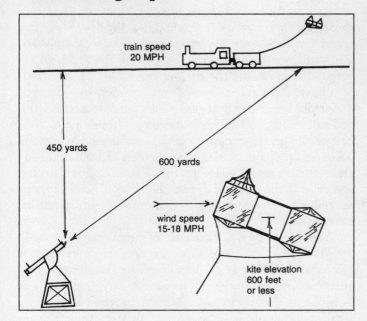

train speed
20 MPH

450 yards

600 yards

wind speed
15-18 MPH

kite elevation
600 feet
or less

To determine antiaircraft effectiveness, machine gun hits were measured against those of forty-eight riflemen. *Source:* original drawing.

the proper mixture of really good shots (eight men), fair shots (twenty-eight), and duds (twelve).[11]

A Vickers machine gun, set up to supply competition, was operated by an expert. However, it was handicapped by a homemade gun mount, for the army issue device couldn't be elevated sufficiently to reach an airborne target.

The riflemen, firing offhand, were permitted seven firing runs.[12] Sometimes notice was given of wind speed (15–18 MPH, against the kite). Sometimes orders were given concerning range and deflection settings. In the course of two days of shooting, some 1,587 rounds were fired. There were eight hits.

The machine gunner was given full advice and three firing runs.[13] He got off 585 rounds, and registered three hits.

In short, whether rifle or machine gun, each weapon hit the critical portion of an airplane target once per two hundred rounds fired. Surely no sensible reconnaissance pilot would loiter about, patiently waiting for two hundred rounds to arrive. Conclusion: small arms antiaircraft fire was merely one more slight hazard, offering a marginal threat to aircraft.

Henderson and O'Gorman could breathe a bit easier; plans for an Air Service could proceed. However, aspects of the data were troubling. For one thing, the distance to the target was enormous. The range employed, a minimum of 450 yards, was well known to be beyond the ability of average shooters facing the simpler task of holing a stationary target. Indeed, the British Army traditionally employed a fourfold larger target at 600 yards, as compared to 400, and still measured a substantial drop in shooting effectiveness at the greater range.[14] Perhaps the chosen kite range was a fair approximation to the approach of a snooping aircraft, but it's also possible that the range choice reflected somebody's thumb on the scale, along with a conscious or unconscious determination to demonstrate antiaircraft ineffectiveness.

Also disturbing was the matter of target speed. Certainly 20 MPH was much too slow, for contemporary aircraft offered 60 MPH. Did the handicap of extreme range balance the bonus of low target speed? No easy judgment was possible. If the results were skewed by choice of range, what range should have been used? In 1912 there was no answer. Indeed, exploration of the entire small arms antiaircraft concept seemed hopeless to many, including the range firing CO, who concluded: "As it is plainly impossible to lay down a simple formula which will quickly solve a [ballistic] problem which includes so many variables . . . further experiment would be a waste of time."[15]

His pessimism was a good fit to the prevailing gloom of artillery officers faced with the problem of marauding aircraft. Speaking in December 1912, Gen. James Grierson glumly noted the problems inherent in hitting a target free to move along any or all of three dimensions, and moving quickly enough to clear its own length in a fraction of one second.[16] Even minor aspects of the problem loomed large: how does one distinguish between friendly and enemy aircraft? How does one practice antiaircraft shooting over a crowded country? He noted that shipborne kites over water had failed—launch and retrieval efforts proved impractical. Then, how can one shoot straight up without suffering casualties from returning shells?

There were many more difficulties in Grierson's depressingly long list. A reporter concluded: "It would be more by accident than design that any man-bird is likely to get winged in flight during war."[17]

Although 1912's ground-to-air threat seemed tiny, the air-to-air possibility remained worrisome. By 1913 the Lewis

German Soldiers Try Their Hand

Firing at an enemy aircraft on the Russian front, summer 1914. *Source:* Baer, ed., *Der Volkerkreig,* vol. 2, 69.

machine gun was in full Belgian production and, at 26 pounds gross, a suitably light choice for an airborne weapon.[18] Throw in a reasonably jam-free performance, a 47-round magazine capable of being replaced with one hand, and the gun seemed most practical—but was any aircraft machine gun really practical? Given aircraft so light as to dip and bank in response to faint gusts, how could accuracy be maintained when experiencing gun recoil? Would quickly changing distances to the target or ground prevent accurate estimates of target range and elevation? In sum, how accurate was fire from an aircraft?

The necessary test was arranged by placing a Belgian Lewis gun expert aboard a British Grahame-White pusher biplane. A jury-rigged seat immediately above the landing gear offered support, with the gun axis pointed forward and down. A square cloth some 25 feet on a side and fixed to the ground served as a target.

Test Firing from the Air

Perched above the landing gear, an expert Lewis gunner prepares for a shooting test. *Source: Flug*, December 1916, 277.

In the course of an afternoon, the expert emptied ten drums of ammunition (470 rounds) at ranges between 200 and 500 yards, all while flying head-on to the target at less than 500 feet of altitude. He scored 280 hits, yielding an on-target effectiveness of about 60 percent, a truly large value quickly announced to the press.[19] So large an effectiveness was especially impressive to those aware of the dismal antiaircraft small arms results.

However, when the monster target area is compared to the smaller silhouetted area considered vital, as in the sketch following, it's obvious that no fit existed, for the

Army Checks It Out

The corresponding American trial yielded about one-third hits on a huge target. Conclusion: hits were easy—if the target was large and immobile. *Source: L'Aerophile,* August 1, 1912, 357.

scaled target area—equal to everything within the outer thin lines—was some twenty-nine times the critical area. Hitting the bloated target was all too easy and implied little about combat success. Certainly no comparison was pos-sible with the results of the kite experiment.

Aside from target area differences, the moving kite presented a difficult "crossing" shot requiring a large offsetting deflection. The kite also experienced a stiff side wind at right angles to the shooters, another major complication, lowering kite-shooting accuracy. In contrast, the Lewis gunner had no deflection corrections to confuse matters. Elevation was a problem, but not windage. He simply fired straight ahead.

Given the "apples versus oranges" nature of the shooting trials, was there really a clear winner? In real life, decisions are frequently forced by lack of time. As given by Samuel Butler II, "life is the art of drawing sufficient conclusions from insufficient premises."[20] In 1912–13 an assessment was required concerning aerial gunnery—was it a menace or not? O'Gorman performed his calculations and conferred with Henderson. Their decisions reflected the shooting trials, Henderson's reconnaissance background, and the short life anticipated of primitive aircraft in the

Target— Critical and Non

The critical portion (in silhouette) covered only a small part of the huge target. Result: each hit required interpretation. *Source:* original drawing.

The British BE2a

The British all-purpose
cooperation machine,
as presented by a fasci-
nated Austrian journal.
Source: Flug, July 1913,
313.

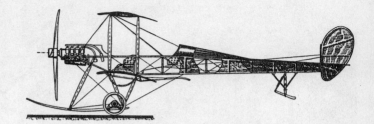

field. Conclusion: air-to-air combat was labeled a small but
significant problem, and ground-based antiaircraft fire was
set aside as a minor nuisance.

History has ruled otherwise; as noted, within a few
years many thousands were to be downed through air
combat. The prewar crystal ball was cloudy indeed.

At the time, in Henderson's view, what really counted
in war was observation, not shooting down the occasional
enemy machine. If some few machines were lost to enemy
fighting machines, so be it. An extremely high wastage in
war was expected in any event. As given by then Capt.
Frederick H. Sykes (later Maj. Gen.) in April 1913: "It
would seem probable that no aeroplanes or engines and
few pilots and observers will last more than three or four
months on active service."[21]

To some extent the casualties would reflect direct combat, but most casualties would result from a lack of necessary flying skill, simple exhaustion, poor judgment, and
mechanical breakdown. At a time when spin recovery was
unknown and stall performance marginal, flying accidents
took an enormous toll. With the aircraft available, "bat-
tling for even 20 minutes through a difficult wind is an exhausting task."[22] Fatigue and bad design were seen as the
airman's true enemies.

As for combat, command of the air would be an obvious boon, but all logic went against such hopes. As Sykes
noted, "A fighting machine with its passenger, gun, ammunition, and possibly light armor, is a heavy machine."[23]
Its supposed prey, the single-seater scout, was inherently
lighter, faster, and more maneuverable. Given the freedom
to dodge about or flee, the light scout had almost no
chance of being hit by a heavyweight. If scouts came and
went as they wished, command of the air couldn't exist. In
short, it was impossible to rule the skies.

Wouldn't scouts attack opposing scouts? As Henderson

The Improved Version: BE2c

1915 version; inherently stable and highly vulnerable. *Source:* original photo, IWM, London, United Kingdom.

saw it, they wouldn't, for, "Their business is scouting, not fighting; they are not equipped for fighting . . . if they are determined to fight, they must get to very close quarters. If the machines are at all equally matched in speed or handiness [i.e., maneuverability] the scouts might maneuver round each other for an indefinite period, missing each other with pistols. . . . The use of [heavier] weapons on a craft not designed for it will be very difficult."[24]

If fighting involving scouts was so unlikely, what was the purpose of the fighting machine? Why did Henderson advocate the development of such an aircraft?

There were a number of prospective uses: to oppose enemy fighting machines, to serve as a means of point defense by fending off ground or aerial invaders, and to attack enemy airships. These were useful functions, but lacked the priority he accorded to reconnaissance. In Henderson's estimation, good scouting could win a war by spying out enemy plans. By comparison, fighting machines could play only a minor role.

Whatever Henderson's doubts, perhaps future scouts would use guns heavier than pistols. Certainly the newly developed Lewis gun seemed a likely choice. O'Gorman pondered the act of firing a machine gun from the BE2—his projected scout and army cooperation aircraft. Given a tractor engine and propeller up front for efficiency, an awkward question emerged: could a machine gun be fired through the propeller without destroying the blades, forcing the plane to land?

Thought alone couldn't supply the necessary yes-or-no answer. O'Gorman believed shooting through the propeller disc relatively safe, because "a large percentage of the shots might miss the blades altogether." In opposition was Capt. S.R. Rice, who reasoned, " . . . propellers, when revolving, are more liable to be hit than when at rest . . . if they move extremely fast, more than one blade might be hit with the same bullet."[25]

A test was necessary. An old Gnome engine and propeller along with 784 rounds were sacrificed in 1912–13 to learn that shooting damage to the propeller was extensive. Firing freely through the propeller disc has been frowned upon ever since.

Although the case against unrestricted shooting seemed clear, the edict's price was stiff—for the slow BE2, prevented from properly defending itself, became easy wartime game. The edict's wisdom continued to haunt shooters even after the war. A new test was arranged in 1920. This time, large bullet holes (.50 caliber) were drilled through wooden propellers while stationary.[26] The holes were arranged in a nicely perforated fashion, suggesting postage stamps or toilet paper. Run up to top speed and more (2,000 RPM) while drawing as much as 350 HP, we intuitively anticipate the blades to tear off on the dashed line. Instead, nothing happened.

The experimenters backed off, noting that perhaps shooting at the blades while in motion changed the game.[27] Perhaps. It's also possible that the prewar test results were viewed in far too conservative a fashion—given a slowly turning four-bladed propeller, even heavy damage to one blade didn't necessarily mean a forced landing.

However, this hindsight wasn't available in prewar days. O'Gorman accepted the negative result derived from his own tests and moved on. In July 1912, using discrete officialese, he announced: "a further program of full-scale work . . . including the construction of different types, in order that their relative advantages and characteristics may be examined."[28]

There were indeed radically new concepts to be tried. First, in line with Henderson's views, a machine so fast that nothing could touch it—a truly fast scout.[29] Next, a greatly improved version of the well-regarded BE2 scout. If given automatic stability, most of its fatigue and piloting error problems would vanish.[30]

Unfortunately, the super-fast scout never came out of development. The stable version of the BE2 did so in the

Holed Propeller Tests

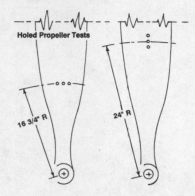

Holed Propeller Tests

16 3/4" R

24" R

When it no longer mattered, test results showed no breakage along the dashed line— or anywhere else. *Source:* original drawing.

The Inverted Dive

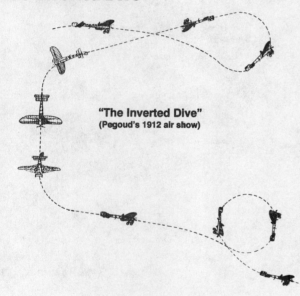

"The Inverted Dive"
(Pegoud's 1912 air show)

Before the war, air show pilot A. Pegoud's routines pointed to the ease of evasion, if under attack. *Source: Flug,* December 1913, 573.

form of the BE2c, and proved a true workhorse, only to be done in by that very air combat denigrated by Henderson as profitless.

How could Henderson have been so far wrong? How could the slight nuisance of one hit per two hundred bullets turn into a menace capable of nearly destroying the Royal Flying Corps?

As the prime means of preventing success in aerial attack, Henderson was betting on evasion—a tactical possibility not offered to the kite in the shooting tests. Lacking

Shooting over the Propeller

Those fearful of shooting through the propeller developed an 'over the top' solution. It failed: too much drag and turbulence for accuracy. Source: *La Domenica del Corrierre*, October 1914, front cover. (inset) Burda, *Fuenfzig Jahre Motorflug*, 64.

any possibility of maneuver, the kite results were incomplete, tending to favor the shooter. Air show maneuvers had shown the military what was possible. Almost every aerobatic maneuver known today had been mastered and demonstrated by France's Alphonse Pegoud in 1912. True, practitioners were few, but the necessary skills were there to be learned.

To the military, Pegoud's endlessly changing orbit defined an impossible target. To these skeptics, the proper odds were not one in two hundred, but one in millions. In other words, given high maneuverability, the chance of downing a scout appeared negligible.

It wasn't so. Given the right attack aircraft, the proper weapon and a modicum of skill, scouts were downed, if not easily, then with acceptable difficulty. Much depended on the right weapons. Which was best suited for bringing down an enemy scout?

2

The Choice of Weapons

IT WAS AN UNHAPPY CHOICE. PISTOLS, carbines, shotguns, rifles, machine guns, cannons, and a nonrecoil gun were all tried. None really satisfied. Each offered enough virtues to attract advocates; yet, disturbing disadvantages soon sent disappointed users elsewhere. Machine guns, certainly the most widely used weapon, were accepted reluctantly and with little respect; indeed, cannon support was strongest among those who used the machine gun best—the top French and Belgian aces.

Doubts and complaints about air war weapons started even before the war, centering on machine-gun drawbacks. British intellectuals W. Arthur Barr and Frederick W. Lanchester damned its rifle-sized cartridge as unsuited for the task.[1] The standard service .303 bullet virtues—long range, high hardness, and compactness—were sensed as useful for the foot soldier but profitless or even dead wrong when employed in a weapon designed to bring down airplanes.

As they saw matters, long range itself was pointless given the severity of the aiming problem; if hits were unlikely at more than 100 yards, why worry about range? Concerning hardness and penetration, they visualized bullets as passing right through the basic wooden airplane construction and continuing on their way, doing little or nothing to bring down the machine. Finally, compactness and low bullet weight offered no advantage when carried in a machine the size and weight of an airplane.

As for the narrow stream of bullets itself, Barr saw it as a foolish approach, attempting "to hide an inherent lack

Barr's Argument

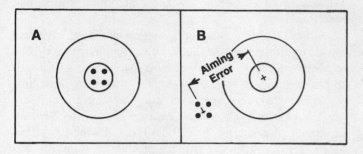

Tight groups (A) are a poor idea; for if given a large aiming error (B) every bullet is bound to miss. Source: original drawing.

The Moris Bullet Catcher

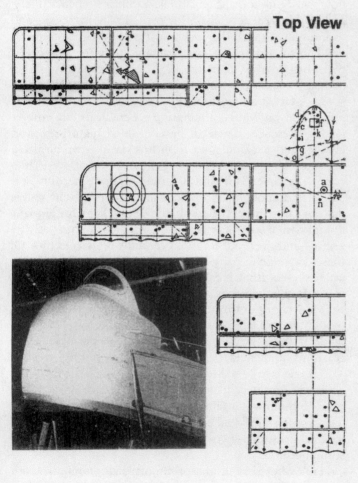

Top View

(from top: upper wing, nacelle and lower wing, elevators and rudder; only left side shown) Some of the 400 harmless hits received by a Henri Farman pusher in the course of 253 hours spent as an artillery spotter and trench bomber. Source: (drawing) *L'Aerophile*, August 15, 1915, 171–73; (photo) original, same Farman type, Canada Aviation Museum, Ottawa, Canada.

of accuracy behind a fog of vain repetition."[2] In other words: should you miss with the first bullet, you'll miss with the last.

Although these complaints suggest whining, each had some logical support. As the war increased in intensity, bitter experience showed how difficult it was to hit a vital spot and how slight a stopping power was offered by most hits.

As an extreme example of gun ineffectiveness, there was the case of Capt. Albert Moris,[3] French Air Service. Equipped with an ancient (1912) Henri Farman airplane, Moris was nominally an artillery spotter. In reality he was much more, aggressively bombing and strafing anything that moved, all from a negligible altitude. To increase his bomb carrying capacity, he flew without a gunner, somehow managing to attack balloons, monitor French artillery, and bomb trenches, all on his own. Easily identified and thoroughly disliked, he drew most every type of counterfire known, from rifles and machine guns to shrapnel at point-blank range, all in late 1914. Although his basic task had nothing to do with air combat, he was involved in seven different air fights as the German Air Service slowly focused in on Moris, attempting to eradicate his embarrassing presence. Unfazed, he continued his private war, energetically accumulating fresh hits on his own airplane, each carefully patched and marked.

At the time, 100 to 150 hours of frontline duty was considered enough for any machine, even without visible damage, but the ever-determined Moris kept his airplane going until Henri Farman #123 reached a total of 253 hours—and over four hundred carefully registered hits. Of these, more than forty-seven struck his bathtub-type nacelle, some within inches of the pilot. His fuel tank was pierced, but there was always enough left to reach home. Bullets went right through critical structural members, but by piloting his stricken machine ever so gently, he always made it back. He was never injured; he never failed to reach his home field.

On the face of it, Moris was proof of the basic invulnerability of any decent aircraft to the menace of firearms. Moris himself was no inspired aerialist. An elderly, nonathletic, professional soldier with many years of prewar service, he possessed two virtues: great determination and stunning luck.

Following six months of almost daily combat, Moris turned in HF #123 as war-weary. Few would disagree. Unhappily, a few missions more, and he was dead in his brand-new aircraft.

Was it all luck? Some embittered fighter pilots thought so. Lieut. Arthur P. F. Rhys-Davids, capable of putting a bullet into Richthofen's friend K. Schaefer (30 victories), believed that once a basic knowledge of the fighting game was acquired, all was a question of luck and stray bullets.[4] In this view, one man was as good as another and only the gods decided victory or defeat. Perhaps, but the intellectuals saw the importance of luck as arising largely from the absence of thought. Given enough thought, one side would produce better hardware or tactics, greatly improving its "luck."

Although there was something to Rhys-Davids's disillusioned view, the intellectuals also had a point. Consider their arguments in detail.

First, the .303 rifle bullet. As compared to the standard auto pistol .45, the pistol bullet was given much less energy when fired. Moreover, its large diameter and rounded lead nose helped expend most of that energy upon arrival. Little was wasted on flashy, pointless penetration. Instead, the limited energy available was invested in breaking or stopping whatever it struck. In contrast, service rifle caliber bullets were guaranteed to penetrate through "some 4 ft. of deal or pine."[5]

As most airplane members were only an inch or so in thickness, the practical result of most hits was to slightly slow the bullet as it passed right through the member and out the other side, free to speed away. The resulting small hole was rarely sufficient to cause structural failure.

Obviously, a strike in a vital spot was quite a different matter. However, as Moris demonstrated, there were few vital spots. Rather than spraying tiny bullets and hoping for a rare lucky hit, the shooter's task could be more easily accomplished by destroying ordinary structure with the right type of bullet. The necessary technology was available; big game hunters had used large, expanding lead bullets for years with the deliberate purpose of decreasing penetration and increasing stopping power. Why not apply the same concept to the downing of aircraft?

One believer was Lieut. Willi Coppens, thirty-seven victories, Belgian Air Service. Angered by "tiny machine guns" requiring "too great a nicety of aim," he pressed for an 11-mm version (roughly .44 caliber) of the Vickers machine gun. Rushing a prototype gun into combat, he

Lewis Gun, Front Mounted

found it "invaluable" for it brought his ninth and tenth victories at a total cost of six 11-mm bullets.[6] However, it was then June 1918, and too late. The big bullet played no significant part in the air war.

Next on the intellectuals' list of condemned notions was the very concept of precisely aimed bullets, to be eliminated in favor of a much preferred shotgun approach. As background, hundreds of years of bird hunting had shown the superiority of shotguns to rifles. If the machine gun were essentially a quick firing rifle and enemy planes merely larger, faster birds, wouldn't some form of automatic shotgun make a better weapon?

A shotgun barrel lacks the usual spiral means of rotating passing bullets. As a result, projectiles are launched without spin. The resulting trajectory is low in predictability because each of the small balls or pellets issuing from the gun goes its own way, lacking the memory of trajectory conferred by spin. The only certainty is statistical: given enough shot, we can expect a broad distribution or pattern tending to fill a circle. With increasing range, the pattern becomes ever larger. The expanding pattern means zero chance of putting each and every bullet into the bull's-eye; instead, the shotgun shooter seeks to shred the target.

Shotgun aim is less demanding. When the shot pattern is large enough, even badly aimed rounds are likely to yield some hits, if given a huge target—and airplanes do make huge targets. Scaling up a shotgun to airplane shredding size, Lanchester designed a 75-mm mortar capable of fir-

Twin Vickers Guns

Standard issue for the Camel, side-by-side mounting implied a high rate of fire. *Source:* original photo, RAFM, Hendon, London, United Kingdom.

ing a load of more than one hundred lead balls, each sized at 0.5" diameter.[7] At 50 yards range, the circular pattern was 20 feet across, enough to assure some hits even if the aim was a bit off.

However, two serious drawbacks overruled use: the weapon was of the single shot type and secondly, achieving the correct 50-yard position before firing imposed an enormous aerobatic burden on the user. Lanchester put it aside. Only those who truly despised machine guns continued to pursue the mortar possibility.

One such was Willi Coppens. He pressed for a much lighter device capable of throwing thirty-two lead balls, each of about 0.65" diameter.[8] As before, the mortar could be loaded only on the ground—a disturbing disadvantage—and nothing came of it.

The prospect of shredding the other fellow by firing one round was all very well, but to be left defenseless thereafter was unacceptable. The attacked enemy might own as many lives as Moris, or possess the allegiance of vengeful friends. One-shot weapons wouldn't do.

Why, then, wasn't the machine gun the answer? Aside from the matter of bullet size, why did so many aces turn against the quick-firing and automatic-reloading machine gun? Most rejecting the machine gun were reacting to personal frustrations. These were largely of two types: malfunctions and aiming errors. Later chapters deal with aim. Consider stoppages, and especially why stoppages resulted in users so angry as to be willing to forgo machine guns.

Lanchester's Mortar

Designed to shred an airplane at a 50-yard range, it lacked a fast reloading capability and so, never saw action. *Source:* original drawing.

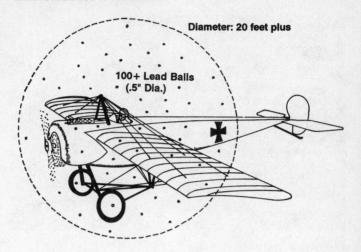

Diameter: 20 feet plus

100+ Lead Balls
(.5" Dia.)

Shooters knew their machine guns to be complex assemblies of tricky parts. Every course of instruction offered some takedown and reassembly experience, with emphasis on stoppages and fast cures. The unexpected part was the realization of how frequently even the best regulated guns refused to work, and of how little there was to be done about it once at lubricant-freezing, oxygen-poor altitudes.

Engines also offered many problems, but though fliers cursed incompetent mechanics and manufacturers, few worked on their own engines. It seemed too much to both fly and repair. Yet most aces worked over their own guns. Many inspected every single cartridge, perhaps with apologies to the armorer, but doing so anyway because their lives were staked on the soundness of each cartridge.

The establishment did offer some support to worried shooters. British Royal Navy Air Service (RNAS) squadrons maintained an official inspection test jig consisting of a spare gun barrel pointed straight down, along with approved instructions: "Drop the cartridges, one by one . . . if they go home they are satisfactory and can be loaded into the magazines."[9]

The test was of some use, for those cartridges refusing to drop all the way home were oversized or bent. However, this test was to cartridge health as a military board examination was to soldiers' health—strong in an easily checked detail, weak in all that was passed over. There was no test for split cartridge cases, corroded brass, defective primers, or undersized parts. It was all up to the inspector's

How Often Did Guns Jam?

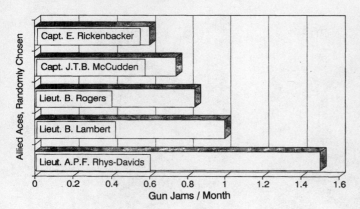

Aces experienced roughly one instance of a jammed gun per month. *Source:* original drawing. Data input from biographies: Rickenbacker, *Fighting the Flying Circus;* McCudden, *Flying Fury—Five Years in the RFC;* Rogers, *Yankee Ace in the RAF;* Lambert, *Combat Report;* Revell, *Brief Glory.*

Hump Firepower

Twin synchronized Vickers guns were faired neatly into the Camel's hump, offering a sturdy aggressive force at a low cost in drag. *Source:* original photo, RAFM, Hendon, London, United Kingdom.

intuition and mood. Not surprisingly, after a stoppage or two, most shooters preferred to do their own inspection.

The jammed gun issue never ended. Approximately once per month, in combat, one or both guns would refuse to fire, usually leaving the shooter defenseless. Truly odd were those many occasions when a paired Lewis and Vickers machine gun would fail simultaneously, though independent in design, location, and means of triggering. Simultaneous jamming of unrelated guns (e.g., SE5a) suggested lubrication failure owing to the extreme cold of high altitude, or perhaps a literal freezing as cloud droplets turned to ice.

The Navy's RNAS preferred one each Vickers and Lewis. However, twin Lewis guns were sometimes substi-

Two guns of separate design seemed unlikely to jam at the same time. However, not so, for climatic conditions that froze one, froze the other. To reload remote Lewis gun (a), use was made of rail (b) to slide it down, so that drums could be changed, and then the gun was pushed back into position—all while flying combat maneuvers. Not easy, that. Source: original photo of replica flying SE5a, Biggleswade air show, United Kingdom.

tuted for special missions, as in the Camel, successful as an anti-zeppelin interceptor.

Although weather problems were real, many more jams reflected the inability of old gun designs to adapt to the newer smokeless powders. Both Vickers and Spandau guns were descendants of Maxim's original design, all born in black powder days. With the advent of smokeless powder came less smoke and much more gas pressure, serving to add muzzle velocity and flatten trajectory. These were all useful traits. Unfortunately, the new, higher internal gas pressure decayed slowly after firing; certainly much more slowly than with black powder. On the one hand, when it came time to eject the fired cartridge case, a great deal of pressure still existed in the barrel, acting to press the case against its seat. Ejecting a case forcibly held in place by gas pressure was not a simple matter. On the other hand, waiting about until the gas pressure dropped off would disappoint users seeking a high firing rate, for the longer the wait, the lower the cyclic rate. An important either-or design decision was necessary and the winning design consideration was a high firing rate. The price was an awesome number of jammed guns.

To eject a brass case pinned to its firing chamber by gas pressure took a most determined yank. Extreme force was available to gun designers and they had little difficulty in

How to Reach a Remote Gun: Camel

The Navy's version of the Camel used a remote Lewis gun reloaded by means of a hole in the upper wing. Swinging the gun down permitted reloading. *Source:* original photo of Camel 2F.1, Canada Aviation Museum, Ottawa, Canada.

assembling the necessary lobes, cams, and catches. The difficulty was in the brass case. Offering no match for the extreme loads of expulsion, the thin brass tended to rip apart. At high altitudes, cold temperatures lowered the strength of the basic brass metal and froze whatever grease might have been available to serve as a friction-reducing lubricant. The effect was to further increase the already large

Lewis Gun Innards

The design was light in weight, low in recoil, and independently mounted (no cartridge belt). However, cons included jams, drum changing, and inability to accept a synchronizer. Source: original drawing with much input from *Flight*, December 6, 1913, 1333.

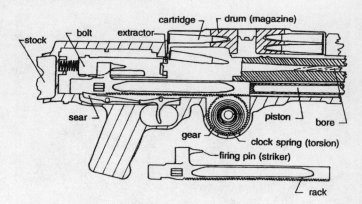

yanking force while simultaneously reducing the cartridge case's ability to withstand yanking stresses. The result was inevitable—broken cartridge cases.

Actually, a fractured case didn't matter—so long as every bit of it was ejected. Difficulties arose when bits were broken off and left behind. Then the next round to enter would wedge the broken bit between cartridge and firing chamber. The bolt couldn't close and, as a safety measure, the gun couldn't fire. The result was a severe jam. There was still a chance: working the charging handle might eject a broken cartridge case. However, even a few pumps of the Vickers charging handle meant disconnecting a feed belt, and then hooking it up again, a matter of additional lost time. As a last straw, the removal process handled broken bits ineffectively and it could take eight or more tries to get all the pieces out.

Consider the shooter's mind-set. His attack has failed, along with his guns. An aroused enemy is out for blood. In the midst of life-threatening combat, the shooter is to unhook feed belts, work the charging handles, and then hook up the feed belts, only to discover that there were apparently more broken bits inside the firing chambers and the cursed guns still won't fire. . . . One can easily picture the rage of shooters afflicted with gun jams.

Finally, there was a monumental form of jam in which the wedging action proved so solid and complete that the charging handle itself was stuck. In this instance, the classic Lewis #4 jam (of 6), official advice was to disassemble the gun "while the obstruction is picked out with the point of a bullet or the spike of a knife."[10] The grim upshot of

A Lewis Drum Underside

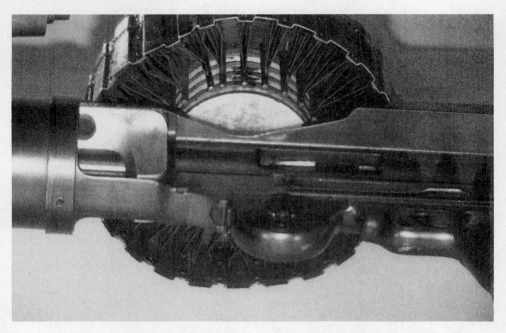

the jam itself—defenselessness—wasn't mentioned, nor was the means by which a jam victim was able to find sufficient peace to disassemble his gun.

The remaining jam types resulted from wear, breakage, and improper adjustment of an extremely complex mechanism. In choosing between the Vickers and Lewis, the gas operated Lewis was likely simpler than the recoil operated Vickers, but even a quick summary of Lewis working concepts, as illustrated, shows an ample opening for Murphy's Law to work its chaos.

Our drawing shows a shortened Lewis in section. A full riflelike stock normally extending to the left, and a conventional barrel extending considerably to the right have been clipped. The bulk of the working parts remain; it is here that most malfunctions originated.

Pulling the trigger lowered the left end of the sear, freeing the rack. Driven forward, or to the right, by the torsion clock spring, the rack (see lower detail) carried the bolt along. After a slight motion the bolt intercepted a cartridge falling from the indexing drum and rammed it home into the breech. Continuing to drive forward, a firing pin mounted on the rack detonated the cartridge primer and

The spring clips held cartridges at the ready, set to feed into the receiver. Bent clips, ice, or dirt meant trouble. *Source:* original photo, Musee de L'Air, Paris, France.

the gun fired. As the bullet moved through the muzzle end of the bore, momentarily blocking the exit, a gas port near the muzzle received great pressure, acting to thrust the piston to the left. The piston motion served to return the rack to its original position; the motion also enabled the rack gear teeth to rewind the clock spring. Most important of all: at the very start of the bolt's return, extractor lugs grabbed the spent cartridge case and ejected it, clearing the way for the next cartridge.

Smooth shooting required the precise timing of very different events, from the release and free drop of a cartridge, initially secure within the drum, to the full return of the rack, propelled by gas. Throughout, operation was strongly affected by working conditions. For example, shooting downward was inhibited by legitimate doubts that the rack would return "uphill." Actually, it would, if the gas pressure port was adjusted accordingly, but the adjustment was complicated by fouling, especially fouling by those strange chemicals arising from tracer combustion.

As all Lewis fire was fully automatic, single shots were impossible. To prevent overheating the barrel, a burst of five rounds was standard, though in combat, ten was more likely and in an all-out crisis the entire forty-seven-round drum could be emptied in five seconds after certain adjustments had been made to the clock spring torsion, increasing the cyclic rate.[11] The process of emptying a drum at one go would almost certainly result in a "blued" barrel, or one whose steel temper had been lost, in turn yielding wildly inaccurate shooting.

Practice paid. Summing up his Lewis gun experience on FE2b aircraft, NCO Arch Whitehouse reported: "I cannot recall ever having had a serious gun stoppage. I may have had, but I was trained to take the necessary remedial action automatically."[12]

Transferred to his RFC task after many months as an infantry machine gunner, Whitehouse started his new life as an airborne gunner with an expertise given to few. To those fortunate few, the Lewis seemed friendly; to most others, it seemed mean and tricky.

As compared to the Lewis, the recoil-based Vickers enjoyed a much longer development period—more than a generation—sufficient to work the bugs out of its unlikely collection of mechanical parts. The result was a fixed gun of twice the Lewis weight, able to fire hundreds of cartridges in short bursts, and all without interruptions of the drum-changing sort. Furthermore, the Vickers could be adapted to firing through the propeller by means of a synchronizer—if not easily, at least it could be done. In contrast, the most determined efforts to synchronize the Lewis, continuing as late as February 1918, ended with the classic inventor's plea: "some redesigning is necessary . . . the failures which occurred were normal."[13] Perhaps, but time was up. The Lewis would always be a flexible, nonsynchronized gun. A belted Lewis also failed to materialize— there was indeed much to be said for the Vickers.[14]

However, along with the powerful Vickers advantages came worrisome disadvantages. For example, the very belt feed that provided continuous fire created horrendous jams, should the hemp-based belt stiffen and freeze at altitude. Combat proved Lewis drums to be as good or better in withstanding extreme cold. A solution in the form of a belt made of metal links, neatly spacing out the cartridges and weatherproof to boot, was developed some two years into the war, but as a disappointed Col. Sefton Brancker wrote to Gen. Hugo M. Trenchard (July 1916): "the articulated belt is made of too soft a metal and the clips are subsequently jamming."[15]

A truly satisfactory disintegrating link belt wasn't available until 1918. The late arrival precluded a significant part in the war; for the most part, Vickers shooters were cursed with the old hemp belt. Then there were difficulties with the Vickers recoil principle itself. Much of the gun's timing employed recoil to trigger a set of precise, built-in delays. Firing reaction sent major parts flying against a toggle and spring, to rebound and return after a vital interval necessary to permit other actions to occur, for example, cartridge case ejection. The time delay value was controlled by the amount of recoil, moving mass size, and spring stiffness. Friction was supposedly a minor factor; yet given a large enough drop in temperature, lubricants failed, friction became large, and the time delay could be far off specification values. The result: one more jam. In this respect, the Lewis was somewhat more fortunate, for its gas-operated mechanism offered a more positive mode of operation.

As both the Lewis and Vickers offered automatic shooting with the same .303 rifle cartridge, competition inevitably arose. Which was best: a flexible gun of limited rounds per magazine, or a fixed gun capable of firing an unlimited supply of ammunition? Although their features were somewhat different, each was intended as the main armament of fighter planes. Yes, each had warts, but on balance which was superior?

Shot Patterns: Lewis Gun Aerial Tests

Test results show sensitivity of Lewis group size to expertise, turbulence, and target movement. Small groups (A) became huge under the influence of turbulence (B) or gun movement (D). Expertise was also crucial (C, D). Drawn to scale. *Source:* original drawing; data input from PRO file #AIR 1/2427/305/19/942.

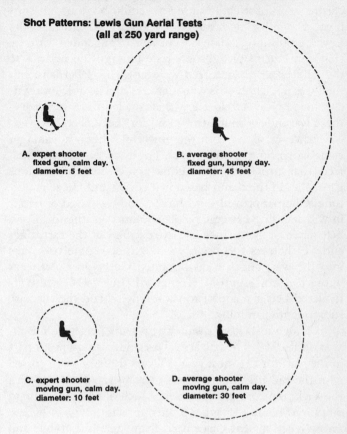

Shot Patterns: Lewis Gun Aerial Tests
(all at 250 yard range)

A. expert shooter
fixed gun, calm day.
diameter: 5 feet

B. average shooter
fixed gun, bumpy day.
diameter: 45 feet

C. expert shooter
moving gun, calm day.
diameter: 10 feet

D. average shooter
moving gun, calm day.
diameter: 30 feet

An early vote (December 1914) went to Vickers, for reasons partly based on the Barr "tight group" logic. Capt. E. F. Chinnery noted: "Lewis guns now in use in the RFC do not appear very reliable and as the magazines hold only 47 rounds, only a very small pattern can be obtained and therefore the gun is not nearly so likely to find the target as the Vickers."[16]

Chinnery was an effective combat pilot, and his observations carried weight. Certainly his reliability comment seems valid, for combat within 1914s low altitudes and nice-days-only policy resulted in the Vickers emerging as the trustworthier gun. All the more striking was the blunder contained in his pattern argument.

Measuring the grouping of shots fired from aircraft required balloon suspension of huge, flag-type targets. A task beyond 1914 technology, pattern results were put in hand by May 1917, when Major B. Hopkinson of Orfordness

Lewis Gun, Flexible Mount

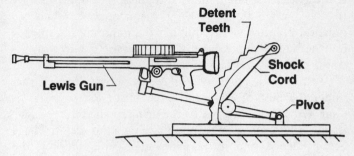

Detent Teeth

Shock Cord

Lewis Gun

Pivot

Detent teeth and a shock cord permitted latching at any desired elevation. Though ingenious, it lacked the rigidity necessary for tight bullet patterns. *Source:* original drawing and original photo DH9, Musee de L'Air, Paris, France.

reported the Lewis group "is rarely, if ever, less than 20 feet in diameter at 300 yards."[17] The resulting pattern was large—only aiming errors larger than 6 feet warranted correction.

It followed that Chinnery was wrong, for his perceived "very small pattern" didn't exist. Exactly the opposite was true—the basic air combat shooting pattern was large, whether the gun was fixed or flexible, with flexible guns supplying much the larger pattern.

All flexible gun mounts permitted a certain play between moving parts and none fully countered recoil force. Given light supporting members, Lewis mounts deflected under air and recoil loads, leading to a large shooting pattern.

Orfordness learned that range, skill, mount design, and turbulence all influenced the shooting pattern. Measuring that smallest diameter covering 70 to 80 percent of all the shots fired—a factor used to discount wild shots—they found range to matter in a straight-line fashion. In other words, twice the range meant twice the group diameter—and four times the bullet dispersal area. In turn, bullet density, or strikes per square foot dropped correspondingly, that is, twice the range meant a reduction of bullet density to one-quarter of the strikes per square foot. From the practical point of view, doubling the range meant spreading the bullets thinly, greatly reducing the chances of hitting a concentrated target.

Testing at a range of 250 yards, it was learned that under the best of conditions (see "Shot Patterns: Lewis Gun Aerial Tests," A, p. 36) the group diameter was a satisfying 5 feet.[18] However, upon adding a "moderate" level of turbulence, and introducing an average shooter, the group diameter expanded to 45 feet ("Shot Patterns: Lewis Gun Aerial Tests," B, p. 36). Even this size could be exceeded, for "bad bumps will spread the group to a much greater extent." In short, Lewis gun shooting at a long range, on a bumpy day, was a questionable activity, offering only the slightest chance of hitting a concentrated target.

Moving the gun about also led to large-sized groups, with shooters of average skill (see "Shot Patterns: Lewis Gun Aerial Tests," D, p. 36) realizing group diameters approaching those seen under turbulence. This was an especially disturbing result, for most gunners were unskilled and most rear gunner targets required a fast traverse. To sum up the entire test series: at 250 yards, most Lewis gunner shooting was pointless. Only those few expert shooters, at a close range, with a fixed gun position, could hope to hit a concentrated target consistently.

Nieuport and SE5a designs made the best of this grim truth by rigidly mounting a Lewis gun to fire forward over the propeller, avoiding the headaches of the Vickers gun belt and synchronizer. The very choice of a Lewis reflected considerable respect, for with the remote gun location came a severe reloading problem. Although pull-down systems were devised permitting a quick drum change, most pilots found it necessary to first leave combat and find a quiet corner—an enormous disadvantage. Still, at 250 yards range, a clamped Lewis generated a group of reasonable size and so hits could be expected; quite unlike the case of the same gun, in the hands of an average rear gunner at the same range, set the task of shooting at a moving target.

Flexible gunnery required some system for varying gun elevation and azimuth. To help carry the weight of the gun, a light tube mount was usually used, with a shock cord supplying countertension through pulleys. Once satisfied, the gun position could be locked. In reality, given a fast-changing combat situation, the gunner couldn't afford the luxury of a locked gun; his strength went into overcoming its inertia and momentum. Accuracy and group size became a secondary consideration.

As for the Vickers, when mounted on a light tripod, ground use yielded small groups—even at long ranges. Putting a Vickers, or twin Vickers, into a Camel flown by a "very skilled pilot" in calm air, resulted in a much broader pattern. Furthermore, the airborne group contained a lower percentage of total strikes, even at a greatly shortened range. Using "on target" bullet density as a measure of merit, and comparing shooting at identical ranges, airborne effectiveness was only about 3 percent of the ground-based figure.[19]

In short, the ability of an airborne Vickers to hit a pinpoint target was much lower than expectations drawn from ground-based experience. Given a split-second firing opportunity, that is, few bullets, the only sure way to hit a small target was to shorten the range.

Of course, the same general increase of dispersion—when airborne—was true of Lewis gun bullets. Moreover, the bolted-down Vickers was easily fed a long belt of ammunition, avoiding Lewis drum reloading problems. As for range and turbulence issues, these were shared by both machine guns. In sum, if at a close range (perhaps 50 yards) both the Vickers and Lewis guns were formidable weapons, with choice dictated by other considerations—reloading and gun motion needs, personal and squadron experience, and finally, the anticipated flying weather.

A sense of Lewis desirability came from its natural target, the German Air Service. When interrogated (April 1916), a prisoner Fokker E-III pilot reportedly "admired our Lewis gun, which is mounted on a German machine when it is captured. The Lewis gun, however, carries too few rounds, in his opinion."[20]

One British observer and Lewis expert, testing the competing Parabellum Aircraft Machine Gun, Model 1913, found it "fairly reliable," but criticized the firing rate as much too slow.[21] A sense of the grass being greener elsewhere, or its opposite—not invented here means no good—animated many such reports. In this case, both guns were good. Certainly, the continued British use of the Lewis as a first-line weapon for several decades beyond the 1914–18 war makes evident a considerable satisfaction.

When mounted on a light tripod (left), a ground-based Vickers yielded a tight pattern. Fired from a Camel (right), the pattern opened up to one of roughly Lewis gun size. *Source:* (left) original sketch; data from Anonymous, *Description of a Light Automatic Gun* (London: Vickers Ltd., 1908), n.p.; (right) original sketch from data PRO file #AIR 1/2427/305/29/942.

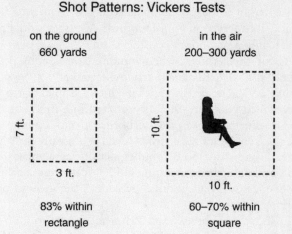

Shot Patterns: Vickers Tests

on the ground	in the air
660 yards	200–300 yards

7 ft.

3 ft.

10 ft.

10 ft.

83% within rectangle

60–70% within square

Yet the Lewis had drawbacks. The limited ammunition supply was one, and early development efforts soon yielded a 96-cartridge drum called a "double." However, it proved unpopular, for its doubled weight demanded too much of shooters bent on changing drums with only one hand. Even the forty-seven-round drum posed a reloading problem. Ace Bill Lambert described one such instance in his SE5a: "I release the Lewis and pull it down to change the drum. As I lift it off I swing my arm out too far. The wind catches it broadside, slaps my right arm down hard on the edge of the cockpit, jerks the drum out of my hand and sends it sailing to the rear. For some seconds I think my arm is broken."[22]

If changing drums wasn't easy, being caught with one's gun down was worse. Lieut. W. M. Fry, a Nieuport pilot noted: "Many is the time I have thrown a full drum overboard and pushed the gun back into position with no drum. If I hadn't done so, I shouldn't be alive to tell the tale. . . . Even in the most favorable condition I had just enough strength to push the gun back into position with a full drum on it."[23]

For a more perfect machine gun, a drum was wanted containing so many cartridges that no change of drums would be necessary. Only then would wrestling with drums in the middle of combat cease and a remote gun location be truly practical. The French Air Service focused on the problem, with their efforts followed by a deeply interested RNAS.

The German Flexible Gun

Parabellum machine gun, Model 1913, carried by a LVG CV. Though good, some German gunners preferred the Lewis gun. *Source:* (photo, above) *Luftfahrt,* April 1918, 16; (sketch, below) Chinn, *Machine Gun,* vol. 1, 315.

By July 1917, a working prototype existed capable of feeding over three hundred cartridges to a standard Lewis gun. It employed as a concept a revised "double" initially, which, when emptied, was automatically reloaded with additional rounds taken from a large flat pan magazine serving as a storeroom. To drive the action, the auxiliary magazine used a clock spring, while the "double" used gas pressure and recoil in the usual fashion. As the gun emptied, the weight and inertia of the magazines changed greatly, and we might anticipate trouble over the timing of cartridge entry—leading to a fierce jam. However, a Lieutenant Tiverton, RNAS, attested to seeing "both these forms [magazines] filled and the full amount shot off."[24] In other words, all three hundred rounds were fired without difficulty.

When an excited Tiverton pressed for production delivery dates, he was told that there were problems in achieving the precision essential for operation—the device didn't lend itself to mass production. Of course, in time . . .

We suspect that a demonstration at ground level in July was one thing, and operation at freezing altitudes in January quite another. Whatever the cause for hesitation, the device never came out of development.

Machine-gun frustrations served to energize development efforts in other directions. The cannon as solution—though obviously heavy and difficult to reload—slowly became more attractive. With the backing of two of France's top aces—Guynemer and Fonck—cannon re-

250-Round Lewis Gun Tray

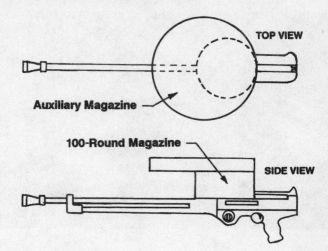

A solution to the drum change problem was claimed by this two-drum device. However, it never entered production. *Source:* original sketch from data PRO file #AIR 1/459/15/312/89.

TOP VIEW

Auxiliary Magazine

100-Round Magazine

SIDE VIEW

search efforts led to prototype devices good enough to enter combat and win. Although the cannon's arrival came too late to seriously challenge the machine gun, it did play a small but real role in 1918; for example, Fonck's victories included seven brought down by cannon fire.[25]

The cannon was of 37-mm bore, or roughly $1\frac{1}{2}$ inches in diameter, placed within an engine's hollow crankshaft. With its breech opening into the cockpit, the cannon barrel ran right through the engine and propeller hub, its muzzle end emerging into free air. This tricky layout had advantages, for no synchronizer was necessary to match gun firing to propeller rates and loading was accomplished by the pilot entirely within the cockpit—without gymnastics. However, manual loading meant a low firing rate; even an improved American copy claimed a rate of only fifteen to twenty rounds per minute.[26] Within the three seconds occurring between shots, a 1918 fighter plane could move through 500 feet; so long an interval between shots encouraged countermaneuvers or escape.

There were other significant problems. The cannon weighed as much as three Vickers machine guns. Manual cannon loading required far more attention than any properly functioning machine gun. An unusually large—and heavy—engine of 230 horsepower was required to house the cannon. In turn, a two-seater SPAD was needed to carry it aloft, with the cannon weight offset by not carrying an observer. The resulting craft lacked the maneuverability of single-seaters.

Cannon-Bearing SPAD Engine

The 230 HP engine housed a 37-MM cannon (right) housed within a hollow crankshaft. Shells emerged toward the reader from the crankshaft bore at the extreme left. *Source:* original photo, Musee de L'Air, Paris, France.

Here was a mixed bag, for the single great advantage of cannon fire—complete destruction of an enemy with a single well-placed explosive round—was balanced with a series of disturbing disadvantages. To most combat pilots, the cannon was an uncertain winner of any cannon/machine-gun tradeoff.

Fonck's unusual style was particularly suited to the cannon. In using his twin Vickers, he took pride in dispatching enemies with the fewest shots possible. Less use of his guns meant fewer jams and more rounds available for his next opponent. Pride was also involved because great skill was required to down an enemy with only a few bullets. As an example, consider the day when he shot down six enemies (September 26, 1918), certainly a striking achievement. However, to Fonck the price was as significant as the deed. It was done "at a cost to me of 52 cartridges"—fewer than nine bullets per downed enemy.[27] He pushed for "8 to 10 cartridges as a maximum, and 3 as typical."[28]

Noting the broad dispersion patterns of airborne machine guns, there was only one way to achieve such a result: he fired from a position immediately behind and in line with his enemy at a range of about 20 yards. At this range, the shot group was small—only a foot or two in size—and with no relative motion between Fonck and his target, great aiming accuracy was possible. Even nine bullets were enough. The hard part was achieving the right position. It was here that Fonck's special quality surfaced—he had a gift for anticipating what any enemy would do next and for being in the right spot to profit from his foresight.

To such a man, typical combat reflected mostly silly tactics. He deemed any strike by incoming bullets as clear proof of inadequacy. He thought the only useful policy was to first achieve the right position, and then to deliver the coup de grace with a few bullets. Few would argue against the virtues of his notion, but the sticky part was in the doing. That he was able to bring it off, time after time, proved Fonck to be a truly extraordinary fighter pilot.

Given a cannon, he continued to use his twin Vickers as sighting devices, checking aim with tracers. Once certain that he was on target, he fired the cannon, blowing away his enemy. As his whole strategy was based on firing once, time spent reloading didn't worry Fonck—in a pinch, he always had the twin Vickers.

The catch was in the requirement of piloting skill sufficient to fling a heavy two-seater about as though it was a light single-seater. Also required were extreme mind-reading skills. Granted these, the cannon was a success.

Fonck was repeatedly pressed for the secret of his ability. Something of a scold, he advocated "regular hours of sleep . . . lead a regular life. Avoid all fuss."[29] His fellow Stork squadron pilots thought otherwise, and Fonck was pushed into a loner's existence. Surviving the war, he worked with friendly writers seeking to capture his genius. Unfortunately, only Benjamin Franklin platitudes surfaced—he owed it all to luck, pluck, and clean living. We think there was more, but no magician reveals his secrets.

Fonck did well with a cannon. However, this is faint praise, for he would have done well without it, or perhaps even better. For the typical fighter pilot, the 37-mm cannon of 1918 was too heavy, too slow to reload, and too demanding of energy better spent in piloting. It would take downsizing to 20 mm and auto-loading to turn the cannon into a weapon suited for the average pilot—an effort requiring many years of development.

Which arms were best suited to bringing down the Red Baron? It was too late for 1914s "time of the carbines" and too early for cannons.[30] A machine gun it would be, and with each type suffering special woes, choice was a matter

Twin Vickers Makes the Front Cover

A Camel nose and twin Vickers guns as featured by *Flugsport* at the time of Richthofen's death. The Luftwaffe was most respectful of these British arms. *Source: Flugsport*, May 1918, front cover.

of voting for the lesser evil. The SE5a went to war with one of each on board—Lewis and Vickers—in the hope that at least one would work when needed. Certainly a back-up gun of a different make would seem a sound insurance policy. Yet, Murphy's Law predicted the actual outcome: if one failed, in all likelihood, so would the other.

Which gun was best? More had to do with the skills and devotion of the squadron armorer than with the ingenuity of factory designers. The pilot's background and especially his mechanical aptitude counted heavily. With the right background—hopefully a few years as an infantry machine gunner, or perhaps work experience as a machinist—the choice of weapons was unimportant. Any would do. With the wrong aptitudes and background, none would do.

At best, machine-gun fire resulted in an outpour of tiny bullets. At reasonable ranges, say 250 yards, a large group resulted. To direct this broad stream, some visual signal of bullet trajectory would be most helpful. Much effort went into tracer development. Yet despite desperate efforts by every warring nation, tracers were more of a problem than a solution. The matter had much to do with sight and optical illusions, for in the air, nothing is easier to gain than false impressions.

3

The Trouble with Tracers

WE SENSE THE AIMING TASK AS SIMPLE.
We imagine each machine gun to offer up a stream of bullets, rather like a water hose spraying water droplets. Intuition tells us that it's only necessary to point the stream
across the path of a target airplane, intercepting the target
as it flies through the stream. Surely, we can't miss; the target will be saturated with bullets. As one RAF pilot employing this approach told the press in 1918, "I . . . ripped
him open from end to end."[1]

Perhaps this was so, but no enemy wreck was available
for damage assessment. As he put it, "I could not see him
actually burst into flames." For that matter, he never saw
the enemy again, and so the pilot's description appears to
be so much nonsense. However, the concept of ripping an
enemy open from end to end remains with us, repeated by
pilots, reporters, and fictioneers. The apparent solution to
the problem of aim makes this approach especially interesting and its reality worth examining.

Great War aircraft machine guns fired at a rate of about
six hundred rounds per minute, or ten rounds per second.
If we imagine an enemy machine crossing in front of a firing machine gun, with the bullet stream perfectly aligned
at right angles to the enemy's path, and taking the target
aircraft speed into account, this firing rate meant that we
could expect only one bullet to strike the enemy machine,
or perhaps two, before it was out of danger. Given the tiny
period of enemy exposure, delivering more than two bullet strikes from each gun was physically impossible.

One or two bullets per gun are few indeed. If two guns
were firing, probability suggests a total of three hits as the

Gravity Drop

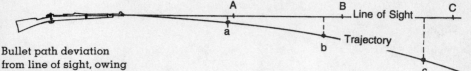

Bullet path deviation from line of sight, owing to gravity drop, was well known. Correction was simple—if one knew the range and had the time to do the computation. *Source:* original drawing.

most likely outcome. An airplane's area is large. Three bullets delivered somewhere along its length were unlikely to bring it down, much less rip it open from end to end. A useful conclusion results: employing a stream of bullets at right angles was a losing tactic. Something more was required. It was necessary to aim that feeble stream, and it was necessary to continuously redirect one's aim as the enemy moved. Indeed, knowing where to aim was the single most important part of aerial gunnery and certainly the most frustrating.

The difficulties posed by the aiming problem proved so great that even years of practice left most men without the knack. Instead, shooters including the Red Baron settled for a firing position requiring the least in the way of aiming skills. If located directly behind an enemy and at 50 yards range, ballistic problems no longer mattered. Aim was simple, for straight ahead would do nicely. However, when faced with a wary opponent, "50 yards and behind" was not easy to come by, and few firing opportunities were of this preferred type. Most shooting encounters were of the crossing type, reflecting spirited determination, but little profit. Although fighting men never gave up on the problem of aim, the area was saturated with pessimism. What was so difficult about aim?

In 1918, ace Maj. Cochrane Patrick described the process of aerial gunnery as "akin to shooting with a rifle a high pheasant doing 100 MPH."[2] He understated the difficulty. For a more complete picture, imagine the shooter as perched aboard yet another bird, also doing 100 MPH while flying independently of the target, and under the extreme stress of imminent death should things go wrong.

To a great extent, the difficulties reflected forces acting to bend bullet trajectory, sending the bullet away from a target so clearly observed and pinpointed by line of sight. The two greatest errors were those of lead or deflection, caused by relative motion between shooter and target, and secondly, those owing to gravity effect. Of these, gravity drop was better known. Although usually not as large as deflection, gravity drop was certainly significant, for it was able to effect a bullet path change of many feet.

In moving over the line of sight range from A to C ('Gravity Drop,' p. 48) the slight lessening of traverse owing to bullet drag was fully understood, as was the ever-increasing trajectory droop, from a to c.[3] All could be computed, and even Newton's simple gravitational formula alone worked reasonably well.[4] For example, at 400 yards range, a predicted 4-foot drop for the standard service bullet was measured and found to be 4.5 feet by Orfordness Armament Experimental Station in the course of studying the drop of every likely service bullet.[5]

Drop value had much to do with the amount of transit time consumed by a moving bullet. Slow bullets permitted gravity's pull to work a bit longer, increasing the drop. The difference between fast and slow bullets proved large; for example, one slow bullet type (RTS) recorded more than three times the drop of a standard Mark VII ball round. In short, high muzzle velocity and streamlining paid, for fast bullets were granted a smaller drop.

The obvious cure for any drop—aiming a bit higher, exactly offsetting the drop—was traditionally applied by means of ingenious gun sights capable of shifting the line of sight by just the right amount. Hunters and riflemen had long employed this scheme, and the process of introducing "elevation" was taught to every army recruit with good results.

However, when applied to aerial combat, new problems emerged. First was the matter of range. Elevation corrections depend on accurate knowledge of range. On the ground, trees, houses, and roads supply a sense of distance. In the air, there are few yardsticks. Range estimates, especially of the split-second sort, were "almost certain to be badly wrong."[6] Even if correct at one instant, fast-changing positions and attitudes were certain to wash out accuracy a moment later.

A second problem was the actual business of making an elevation sight setting. It took time, and in air combat there was no time. Typical elevation correction systems required the precise shifting of a tiny crossbar on a vertical sighting member. Painstaking precision was required, with every shifting and locking move defying thick mittens and frozen fingers. At issue wasn't the superiority of one system over another, but the pitifully slow process inherent in setting all known adjustable sighting systems.

Gravity Drop—Test Results

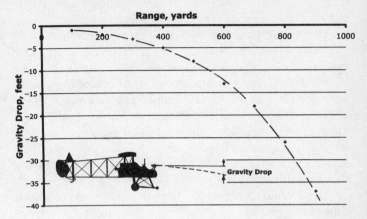

A third elevation problem was the issue of dealing with the vertical. In shooting straight up, no elevation correction is wanted. Gravity drop continues to exist in this instance, but does not influence the trajectory itself. If the bore sight is set straight up, so is the trajectory—a path not at all like the usual curving droop. Only the distance covered is lessened, shortening the altitude achieved, but this is usually unimportant. Much the same is true for straight down—distance is increased, but elevation correction is unwanted. A good sight might be expected to know this and automatically introduce elevation corrections suited to the degree of up-or-down attitude encountered in sighting. In time, inventors would pounce on this special problem. However, no practical Great War sighting device had the necessary degree of intelligence.

To the real difficulties posed by gravity drop were added the much greater errors inherent in the problem of lead or deflection, sometimes called allowance. Although bullets moved at better than twice the speed of sound, passage to the target still required a certain amount of time, during which the target moved on. At an assumed target flight speed of 100 MPH, even that small fraction of a second required for bullet arrival permitted significant motion; at this speed, for each one-tenth of a second of bullet travel time, the target moved roughly 15 feet.[7] To hit accurately, it was necessary to predict this motion and allow for it by introducing the proper deflection.

A realistic, difficult application came from Major Patrick: "Assuming the firer to be stationary and the enemy machine flying across his front, and the firer at 200 yards

Correcting Line of Sight with Lead

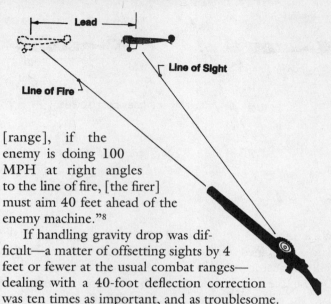

Lead, or correction to the line of sight, attempted to predict where the enemy would be when the bullet arrived. *Source:* original drawing.

[range], if the enemy is doing 100 MPH at right angles to the line of fire, [the firer] must aim 40 feet ahead of the enemy machine."[8]

If handling gravity drop was difficult—a matter of offsetting sights by 4 feet or fewer at the usual combat ranges— dealing with a 40-foot deflection correction was ten times as important, and as troublesome.

Although the concept of introducing deflection was well known to sportsmen and bird hunters, the sheer magnitude of a 40-foot correction was novel and unsettling. Furthermore, even if it proved possible to crank in so large a sight-line shift, there was good reason to doubt the accuracy of the lead calculation itself. In his example, Patrick simply assumed speed and range values, and proceeded from there. In combat no values were supplied the pilot or gunner—each made his own assessment—and everything learned in the Great War suggested enormous errors were likely in the process

The official Orfordness study of enemy aircraft speed assessment by British pilots concluded the process to be "helplessly [*sic*] inaccurate."[9] Faulty range estimation was viewed as partly responsible because one needs an acute sense of distance to translate a tiny moving dot into a speeding enemy aircraft at a known range. Applying the usual poor quality speed and range assessments to Patrick's crossing example, the correct lead estimate could be either twice or half the correct 40 feet, with no hint given the shooter as to which was the more likely. In combat, good men spotted an enemy, calculated a deflection estimate, aimed ever so carefully—and missed by whole aircraft lengths. A few experiences of this sort and most men were understandably eager to find the magic firing spot "50 yards and behind."

Tracer Flaw #1: False Hits

Overrunning a near miss produced the illusion of a direct hit. Viewers couldn't distinguish between a near miss (left) and a hit (right). *Source: original drawing.*

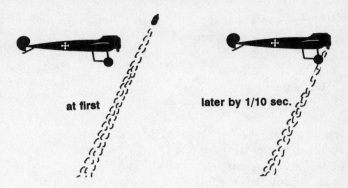

at first

later by 1/10 sec.

What of tracer ammunition? Designed to mark the sky with a combined red flare and white smoke record of actual bullet trajectory, a tracer's whole purpose was to help aim. On the face of it, if shooters could see trajectory and direct it to the target, a bull's-eye was certain. Was it so?

At short ranges—100 yards or fewer—tracers worked as planned. However, there was some question as to need. At extremely short, point-blank ranges, aiming assistance wasn't strictly necessary. Yet tracer use had the negative effect of alerting an enemy initially blind to one's presence—inattentive and altitude frozen—until awakened by the blossoming of smoke trails. Whether small gains in aim at point-blank range were offset by loss of surprise was a matter of judgment.

Over long ranges—where important aiming advantages might be expected—a number of illusions developed, with results that were harmful rather than useful to aim.[10] Consider Patrick's crossing case again. Imagine the shooter to be using slightly too much lead; his bullets pass by harmlessly, a few feet in front of the enemy machine. A split-second later the enemy overruns the tracer smoke signals, all without harm. However, the shooter does not sense the delay behind the apparent collision of target and tracer, for delay times of 0.1 seconds or thereabouts are too short for human perception. To the shooter, bullet and tracer seem simultaneous—he believes himself on target.

The illusion of a hit proved all-powerful. Intelligence officers arguing with shooters wrongly claiming enemy destruction were unable to shake their convictions. Instead of accepting the simple truth—the enemy was untouched—gunners attributed enemy survival to hidden armor.[11]

Tracer Flaw #2: Old News

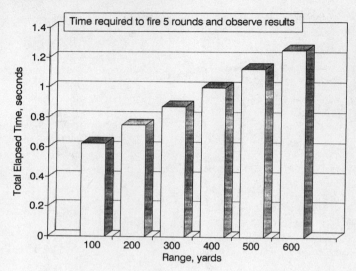

Given a two second firing opportunity, there was no time to wait for a tracer display. Events occurring a second ago were old news. Source: original drawing; data input, see chapter 3, note 14.

The establishment reacted with new instructions: "Tracer is to be used as a guide only if a bullet is seen coming *out* of the hostile machine."[12]

While useful as an illusion-preventing measure, the edict smacked of "let them eat cake"; obtaining a position where bullet traces could be seen emerging from an enemy was far from easy.

A second long-range tracer drawback was the time required for perception and judgment.[13] At a range of 400 yards, bullet traverse required about ½ second. During this elapsed time, five more bullets were fired, and both the firer and target moved on by about 70 feet. At best, tracers informed the firer of his aim some five bullets ago, when his target occupied a very different position in space. Given a fast-changing dogfight, this amounted to old news with information of uncertain value; perhaps pertinent, perhaps worthless. An experienced firer might determine whether his position relative to the target was changing quickly enough to invalidate the necessarily old tracer data. However, inexperienced firers could not, and there was no time for reflection.

A third tracer disadvantage had to do with the likelihood of drawing false conclusions concerning the center of aim. Especially misleading were those tracers highlighting a broad firing pattern.

Tracer Flaw #3: False Center of Aim

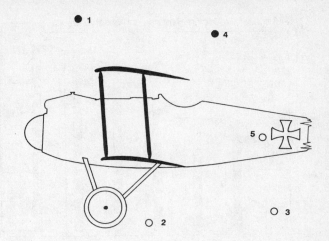

Tracers (filled-in circles) were usually much fewer in number than nontracers (empty circles) and could generate a false impression of the center of aim—here mistakenly sensed as too high. *Source:* original drawing.

No gun repeats its firing trajectory perfectly. In chapter 2 we met those variations in target strike locations testifying to bullet dispersion. In brief summary, when firing from an aircraft, the basic gun-on-the-ground pattern, usually small, was greatly increased by any sponginess offered by the gun mount, as well as by air turbulence. Enormous patterns at long combat ranges resulted. Given expert mechanics, a good shooter, and a calm day, better results were possible, and the above sketch shows a better-than-average pattern at 400 yards.

Although tracer frequency was up to the shooter, most settled for one round of Sparklet in three; the other two being ball and armor-piercing. For example, we might expect a five-round sample to contain tracer (round 1), ball (2), armor-piercing (3), tracer (4), and ball (5). This group would be fired within half a second, a significant amount of time in combat; as given by Ralph Sorely, in charge of drawing up postwar British fighter gun requirements, "It was hard to keep aim at the enemy for more than two seconds."[14] Operating within a 2-second limitation, information received over the first half second was valuable, for something might still be done to change aim. Conversely, anything learned over the last half second was worthless, for the game was about to end. In short, there was tremendous pressure on the shooter to monitor the fewest possible tracer observations, and quickly at that.

Unfortunately, given a large pattern, a good many shots were necessary to locate the center of aim properly. If

Tracer Flaw #4: False Trajectory

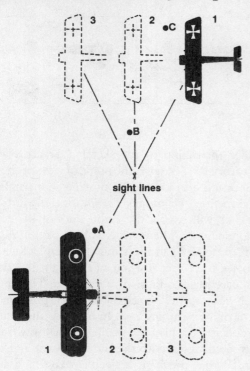

sight lines

Suppose British gunner (1) shoots at German scout (1). Later aircraft positions (2) and (3) result in sight lines 2–2 and 3–3. Bullet (A) initially to the left of sight line 1–1, continues on to position (B) still to the left of sight line 2–2, but then appears to veer (C) rightward of sight line 3–3. The gunner concludes that path ABC is a severely bent dogleg. Actually, path ABC is a near-perfect straight line. *Source: original drawing.*

all five shots could be seen, something useful could be done in the way of sensing general aim. However, with only two tracer trails standing in for a group of five bullets, firers were frequently given a false impression. In this case, though actually well centered on the target, his eyes tell him that he is firing too high. Should he adjust his aim in response, matters will only become worse. In truth, the fault was one of impatience and too small a sample, not of tracer accuracy, but disappointed shooters found it easier to blame tracers.

One more illusion also seemed to point to tracer inadequacy—a matter of apparently curved bullet flight. In this full optical illusion, tracers perceived from a moving aircraft appear to curve off into the distance. The apparent curvature is enormously exaggerated, for actual bullet path curvature is small. Yet, like all tracer illusions, it proved absolutely convincing. In the worst case—shooting broadside at a distant enemy while moving oppositely —the false trajectory curvature was so great as to mock any attempt to aim.

Side View—Tracer Flaw #4

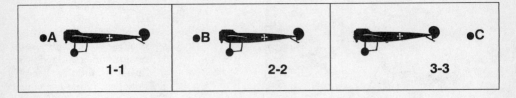

Source: original drawing.

Consider the action in the sketch ('Tracer Flaw #4: False Trajectory,' p. 55) from the point of view of the BE2c gunner. Spotting a Fokker E-III moving in a parallel but opposite direction, he judges that firing leftward of his sight line 1–1 will supply the right amount of lead. He shoots a single tracer. The result is bullet position A. Later, he flies on to point 2, and looking along sight line 2–2 is pleased to see the tracer just left of the sight line at position B, apparently heading for the target. However, on reaching 3, he is startled to see the bullet at position C, far to the right of his sight line 3–3. In his view, the bullet got off to a good start, achieved a promising halfway position, and then veered violently to the right.

If assured that the basic trajectory ABC is a straight line, he reasons that his tracer was an exception: that it was defective in some way. After a few such experiences he may well conclude, along with ace Lieut. Bill Lambert, that "tracer bullets are very confusing and do not always go where indicated."[15] Actually, they did, every time. It's the interpretation of trajectory that proved a bit tricky.

This particular illusion stems from the self-centered nature of the gunner's observations. He has confused position relative to a changing sight line with position relative to the ground. The two are very different. For example, to an observer firing a tracer from a roller coaster, the subsequent bullet trajectory consists of wild gyrations. Yet another observer on the ground will see a straight-line path. For most shooting purposes, the path relative to the ground is wanted; the roller coaster view is useful only after correction for the underlying motions of the car.

While it's easy to spot the gunner's error, prevention was not so simple. One needs a steady reference—a dominant landmark—and air combat offered few. The illusion proved especially powerful at night, when tracers are brightest and all landmarks vanish. Night combat films of World War II vintage continue to offer viewers the curved

Preventing Tracer Fires

Another tracer problem was a tendency for passing bullets to drip burning chemicals on well greased rocker arms, starting engine fires. This Fokker D7 had special troughs (arrows) to prevent such fires. *Source:* original photo, Musee de L'Air, Paris, France.

trajectory illusion at full strength, and a most powerful illusion it remains, defying disbelief.

A natural result of illusions and incorrect usage were endless rumors of tracer failure to represent service ammunition trajectory accurately. However unfair, Lambert's complaint was universal. In reality, by August 1915, British tracers worked properly through a range of 300 yards.[16] Further development carried the range of visibility to 650–750 yards, adequate for most air combat purposes.

The necessary technology was shared, copied, or initiated by the French and Germans. Working toward a universal tracer, with every bullet type carrying a tracer component, German efforts managed to produce an armor-piercing tracer (May 1917) good through 600 yards.[17]

In short, effective tracers were available to every Air Service over the great bulk of the war. Tracer introduction delays were not so much technical as legal and moral, for once the tracer burned off, the residual shell was a hollow shell likely to cause a gaping wound. Such devices were banned by the Declaration of St. Petersburg, signed by the British before the tracer concept evolved.

To the politically sensitive General Henderson, the newly developed tracers seemed both a potential boon and a problem. In August 1915, he queried higher command: "It is probable that the bullet breaks up considerably on impact, and I should be glad to know whether it is considered expedient to take it into use."[18]

In response, he was informed: "As long as it is confined to use as a range finder against aircraft, it is unobjectionable, or at least justifiable."[19]

Although the reply was not quite responsive, it was accepted as approval and tracers were officially on as of the end of August 1915. In time, users came to feel at moral ease with the concept, especially so when the explosive bullet came along, acting to dwarf the perception of human damage caused by tracers.

With use came an appreciation of tracer complexities— tracers could serve the enemy as well as oneself. For example, in one fight British ace William A. Bishop (then Lieut., later Air Marshall) reported: "I let go a burst at my nearest antagonist and saw my tracer bullets hitting the bull's-eye!"[20]

The German pilot reacted by spinning downward through 1,000 feet. However, the spin proved to be a ruse, for he proved more combative than ever until finally, "[I] saw my tracers hitting all around the cockpit . . . he spun right in."[21]

In this case, tracers from an initial poorly aimed burst likely caused the German pilot to put his play-dead ruse into action; here, the apparent "bull's-eye" feedback to Bishop added convincing, totally false support to the act. In the second tracer instance, Bishop's perception of critical damage was correct. In short, tracers could supply useful information, or nonsense, and sometimes both in the same fight.

Management was torn by tracer oddities. Tracer certainly had its uses, and even within the disappointing area of aim there was a clear gain in one case—shooting at a fairly close ground target. Here the ground itself supplied the necessary basic orientation and there was no doubt about the end point, for each tracer struck the ground at the end of its trajectory. For shooting up trenches, tracer worked well.

There was also tracer's incendiary function, acting to set fire to a pierced fuel tank, or to fabric if soaked in fuel or oil. Although true tracers did not make the best of incendiaries, as measured by balloon-igniting standards, they were regarded as better than nothing and so, widely used.

Tracers also worked well as a signaling device. They even served for sending messages to the enemy. Consider this example.

Lightened bombers returning from a raid made an im-

Did Twin Guns Help?

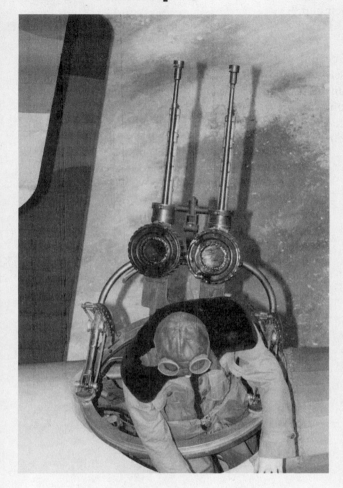

Despair over the aiming problem led to two guns for observers and a new difficulty: controlling gun mass while maneuvering. Breguet 14 shown. *Source:* original photo, Musee de L'Air, Paris, France.

posing enemy, especially if in strong formations. Attacking such a formation was a high-risk business and the usual attacker's plan was not to be seen until too late, a matter of a sly approach from the formation's blind underside. Should this ruse be detected, bomber gunners would fill the air with tracers, not caring about aim, but using the highly visible bullets to advertise their wariness. If the attackers were faint-hearted, proven public knowledge of their failure to achieve surprise would usually prevent an attack.[22]

Management did grant tracer uses, but when it came to air-to-air combat, the many bitter wartime disappointments led Orfordness to conclude:[23] "At longer ranges its [tracer] indications are so misleading that gunners should, for general purposes, be taught to disregard it altogether in their aim."

Here was the clearest possible admission of tracer failure.

If both the hose-at-right angles approach and tracers were useless as aiming devices, what then? There was always the gun-sight possibility, along with its troublesome computation of where the enemy ought to be a fraction of a second later. Could something be done to simplify the business of estimating allowance? Did some gadget hold the answer?

4

Aim and Simple Sights

WITH THE FAILURE OF TRACERS AS A basic aiming concept, gunnery hopes moved on to gun sights. The "try anything" mood embraced devices ranging from the crudest sort of open iron sights to subtle optical devices of the lens and reticle type. Mounts varied from the cheapest clamps capable of securing iron sights to a gun, to sophisticated compensating gadgets offering automatic azimuth correction as an observer swung his gun about.

Every gun sight design attempts to ease the problem of bringing about a meeting between bullet and enemy. To do its job, available technology first required human estimation

Lewis Gun on Vickers Gun Bus (1915)

Early gun sights offered no help in setting deflection and were much too slow at range setting. Source: original photo, RAFM, Hendon, London, United Kingdom.

of target speed, direction, and range. Only when given a sense of how fast the enemy was traveling, his direction, and distance from the shooter, could a Great War sight do the necessary work to assure a hit. The catch was in the input, for stiff accuracy demands were placed on the gunner. Let's consider the input terms, one at a time.

Speed estimation dominated the deflection correction. Take a simple case in which the gunner is stationary—for example, antiaircraft duty—with an enemy crossing the gunner's sight line at a perfect right angle. Let's assume the range information to be perfect, so that the gunner lacks only the correct enemy speed. Spotting the enemy at A ('Why Speed Estimates Mattered,' p. 63), the gunner assigns a velocity intended to produce a hit at B; a task physically accomplished by angling the gun barrel off the sight line by just the right amount—the gun sight's job. If the gunner's estimate is correct, all is well, and a hit is most likely. However, if the gunner mistakenly assumes too low a speed, the plane will outspeed the bullet to arrive at C, with the bullet passing harmlessly behind.

Was it possible for a competent gunner to be that far wrong? The full spread of possible velocities for most World War I aircraft was about two to one, with the high-speed end experienced when in a shallow dive, and low speed developed at maximum climb rates. Few enemy machines offered much in the way of visual clues to speed. Yes, there was a difference in attitude between dive and climb, but the difference was small and if given only a second or two for evaluation, the gunner was unlikely to get it right. Indeed, the official British wartime experience, entirely negative, was neatly summed as "no direct estimate of relative velocity is possible."[1] As a practical solution, the gunner was advised to "assume an average speed" for the enemy—say cruising speed—and to hope for the best.

Next, consider direction. Shooting in the right direction is intuitively sensed as critical to accuracy and we aren't surprised to find direction listed as one of the key sight needs. However, the difficulty of getting it right is unexpected.

Consider the gunner's problem again. This time assume that he knows the enemy's velocity and range precisely, but is mistaken as to heading. Sighting the enemy at A ('Why Flight Direction Mattered,' p. 63), he assumes the flight path to be at right angles to the sight line, as before, and adjusts his gun sight anticipating a hit at B. Instead, the enemy reaches C, and the bullet passes to his front.

Why Speed Estimates Mattered

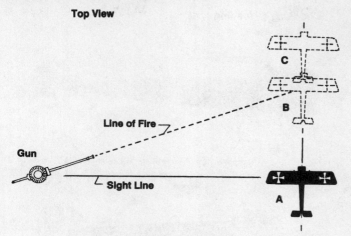

Top View

Assigning too low a speed to a crossing enemy assured a miss. *Source: original drawing.*

Line of Fire

Gun

Sight Line

Why Flight Direction Mattered

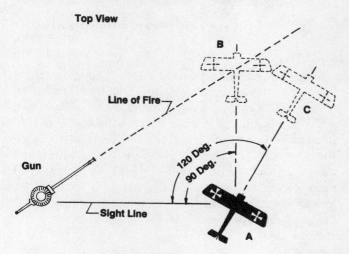

Top View

An angular error in flight direction estimation could mean a complete miss. *Source: original drawing.*

Line of Fire

Gun

120 Deg.

90 Deg.

Sight Line

Is so large an error in estimated direction realistic? Consider the gunner's problem. Crossing enemies appear largely in profile, that is, as side views. As the enemy is assumed to fly at an altitude identical to that of the gunner, a 90-degree crossing results in a perfect side view, as shown.

The true enemy heading—120 degrees to the sight line, rather than the assumed 90—results in the profile shown. The gunner's error is one of confusing the two profiles. There are differences, and the fuselage image does

Which was the correct angle? Gunners were expected to assess an enemy's direction after a few seconds of study—not an easy task. *Source:* original drawing.

Choosing a Heading

Side View

Gunner's View: Enemy at 90 Deg. to Sight Line

Gunner's View: Enemy at 120 Deg. to Sight Line

change a bit—mainly in overall length. Unfortunately, this is a useless measure, for it is too readily attributed to a change of range. Much more useful is the oblique view's gift of two landing-gear wheels and a wing tip—easily identified objects that can't be detected in the right-angle view. Realizing that the sensed distance between wheels is his most sensitive index to angularity, gunners struggled with the problem of judging a difference of a few feet some hundreds of yards away. For example, at a range of 200 yards, given appropriate reductions to scale, the images alter into:

An Oblique View

At 200 yards range, the distance between wheels was the best indicator of flight path angle; (left) perpendicular, (right) oblique. *Source:* original drawing.

In reality, the images didn't exist in stark black and white, as shown, but as muddy-wheel hues against a muddy countryside, further darkened by the wing's shadows. Imagine two dirty wheelbarrows placed a few feet apart on a flatbed truck moving at top speed, two entire football fields away, with all in deep shadow. Permitted a couple of seconds of vision, the gunner's function was to guess at the distance between the barrow wheels. For most men, it was a hopeless business.

Yaw served as an additional source of directional error. Imagine the enemy aircraft (see 'Yaw and Flight Direction,' p. 66) to maintain an oblique attitude to the gunner, as at A, and the gunner to properly sense the oblique angle. Reasoning that the enemy was proceeding to B, he would aim accordingly. However, oblique stance itself need not reflect flight path, for it is possible to point in one direction and fly in another, a process called yawed or crabbed flight. In this case, the true path might well be perpendicular to the gunner's sight line, in the direction of C. Flying in a severely yawed attitude resulted in high drag, with the enemy's speed correspondingly low. As a result, the enemy lagged behind the bullets—once again, the gunner missed.

World War I aircraft were able to maintain yaw angles as large as 25 degrees routinely, an ability useful when crabbing into strong side winds to hold course, or in dumping altitude if coming in to land just a bit too high.[2] Here the extreme drag of sidewise flight, coupled with a nose down attitude, ate altitude and speed. When on final, just off the grass, the pilot swung the nose in the direction of flight, eliminating yaw, and yielding a smooth landing as a reasonable expectation. Savvy pilots, at ease with extreme yaw, used it to confuse gunners.

There were drawbacks. If used at a high angle of incidence, as in climb, there was a good chance of spinning out. Secondly, there was little chance of hitting anything if firing from a yawed attitude—gun sights weren't prepared with yaw in mind. Despite these serious limitations, yaw made for a superb defensive flight path. If one's guns quit in the middle of a dogfight, diving out of harm's way tended to attract followers with functioning guns—working enemies who happened to be better divers. Edging out of the scramble at a high yaw angle attracted less notice and offered at most a puzzling target to determined followers.

Finally, consider range, and the requirement for accurate range estimation. Although the need for accurate enemy speed and directional input seemed reasonable to all, range was more difficult to accept intuitively. Unlike a forward pass in football, where throwing for a precise distance is critical to success, air combat rarely employed plunging fire. Instead, as a simplification, only flat fire was considered effective, and that for only a few hundred yards range. Corrections were then applied for an average amount

Yaw and Flight Direction

Yaw, that is, a sideways or crabbed attitude, lent itself to directional errors. *Source:* original drawing.

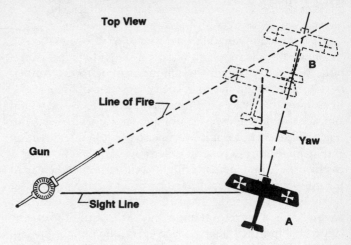

of gravity drop over the curtailed range. In this manner the awesome complications of a forward pass were eliminated. Instead, all shooting was turned into a form of lateral passing, that is, made similar to a short, flat throw. But if the range was short, why worry about getting it right? Does the thrower of a lateral pass take range into account?

He'd better. Consider the "Why Range Estimates Mattered" sketch following.

Here the gunner, seeing an enemy at A, correctly assesses speed and direction values, anticipating a hit at B. However, let's suppose that range is greatly overestimated. In time, the enemy reaches position C rather than B, and the bullet passes behind him.

Range mattered. The simplifying assumptions of flat fire didn't eliminate the necessity for good range estimates. Flat fire concepts were useful in erasing certain hopeless long-range prospects, restricting shooting to ranges offering some chance of a hit—but the need for accurate range estimates remained.

In these examples, only the simplest case has been considered: a crossing enemy at the same altitude as a stationary gunner. In reality, the enemy was probably at a different altitude, may well have been diving or climbing, and the gunner, far from being fixed in space, was likely aboard a violently maneuvering aircraft. Each of these factors greatly complicated the gunner's task of estimating relative enemy speed, direction, and range.

Why Range Estimates Mattered

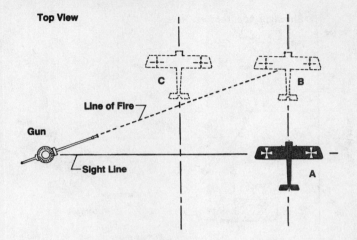

Top View

Line of Fire

Gun

Sight Line

C

B

A

Granted the difficulty, how close did the average shooter come to his target? If we imagine the shooter's center of aim to be his enemy's head at a respectable range of say, several hundred yards, was the chance of a hit large enough to be taken seriously?

British tests of a forward Vickers gun on a variety of fighter aircraft showed range to be a powerful factor in determining accuracy.[3] Given a large, stationary target in the form of a flag suspended from a balloon at altitude, expert pilots ran up high scores at short ranges. At 300 yards or fewer, hits were most probable. However, the likelihood of a hit faded with increasing range, until at 1,000 yards the probability of a hit became negligible.

The basic finding—the shorter the range, the better—is no surprise. Firing results at 400 yards, usually taken by shooters as the largest practical value, were inferior to those at 200 by as much as 50 percent—a considerable drop in accuracy.

Given these findings, the employment of 400 yards as a limiting value for range is understandable; especially so once the enormous size of the target flag is factored in, for it contained seven times the area considered truly vital, that is, 140 square feet of flag as compared to 20 square feet of vital enemy target area. The percent of hits to be expected, given a properly scaled down target, would be much smaller.

Were the final values of accuracy, corrected for target size, good or bad? Official analysts shrugged and moved on after lamenting the extensive training necessary to

Aim and Simple Sights

Why Range Mattered

Pilot-fired Vickers gun accuracy decreased with range. The fall-off was especially steep at shorter ranges. For a sure hit, it was essential to approach closely. *Source:* original drawing. Data from Orfordness final report, PRO file #AIR 1/2427/305/29/942.

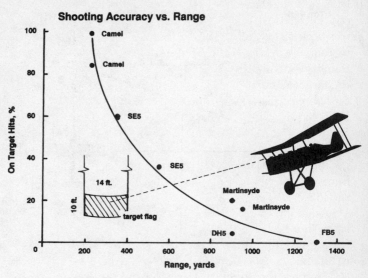

achieve even the measured level of marksmanship. In mock combat "such aiming as has been recorded by the camera is generally bad." However, given "an easy shot" the results "should be no worse than with an observer's gun."[4] Noting the unimpressive record of Lewis gun accuracy we are left with a sense of the extreme difficulty in bringing down an enemy. Whether flying a single-seater or serving as a two-seater gunner, one needed skill, a calm day, a well-functioning gun, a great deal of ammunition, a bit of luck, and hopefully an inept or slumbering enemy.

These were demanding requirements. Satisfying them all simultaneously was unlikely. Those who became aces thrived because their level of skill and determination were much higher than the norm.

Aerial gunnery worked, bringing down many enemies, but it worked reluctantly, cursed by its insistence on correct ranging estimates, and handicapped by the limitations of gun sights. This was no sniper's weapon. Even old hands found it difficult to bring fixed or flexible guns to bear on a target. Why didn't gun sights solve the problem? A look at gun-sight details is useful.

Aerial gun sights started with the knowledge gained through hundreds of years of bird hunting. Experience had shown that rifle sights worked very well for stationary or slowly moving targets, but failed against fast-moving birds.

In rifle target shooting, correctly used sights appear hazy and slightly out of focus, for the main eye effort is concentrated on the target. This sharing of vision works well so long as the target is immobile. However, attempts to follow a fast-moving bird results in a tendency to fire trailing shots as the gunner, unable to cope, lags behind the target. His problem starts with the need for simultaneously seeing the front sight, back sight, and moving bird. Each requires a different eye focus. Difficult to master at any time, the gunner's split-focus internal computer can't compute new corrections quickly enough, should the target bird either speed up or change direction. In short, human computational abilities are too limited to handle the job.

As an alternate solution, fowling shotguns offered no-sight shooting. Instead, the shooter was trained to swing his or her left arm, guiding the muzzle in an arc designed to match the bird's motion. As for sights, British expert shooter and gunsmith Robert Churchill specified: "The shooting man must keep his eye on the bird and ignore his gun."[5] Sights were to be used only after the shell was fired, in recoil, to note the accuracy of aim. Everything depended on a trained link between eye and arm.

As with juggling knives, it worked, if given years of practice. European sportsmen and hunters brought up with this system found it direct, natural, and useful. Application to the problem of shooting down enemy aircraft—without the shotgun—resulted in early French success.

On average, it takes five large-sized buckshot pellets to bring down a single deer.[6] Airplanes were judged an even more resistant target. Instead, the shotgun was replaced with a carbine, employed in the same no-sights fashion. Borrowed from the cavalry, the carbine offered only four shots—one in the breech, three in the receiver—but operation was semiautomatic, with no bolt to work back and forth.[7] Some fortunate shooters were able to bring along their own Winchester model 351 carbines, regarded as a much superior weapon because it never jammed.[8]

All the usual problems burdening air combat accuracy existed for the carbine, plus one more—its short barrel was inherently less accurate than a military rifle. How then could a freely swung carbine succeed in bringing down aircraft? What was the French secret? For an answer consider two combat reports typical of late 1914, "the time of the carbines."

By October, Lt. Perrin de Brichambaut had opted to fly

observation missions in solo fashion, gaining a bit more performance from his Henri Farman "chicken coop" two-seater pusher.[9] As for possible combat, he prepared by arranging a set of heavy rubber bands cut from inner tubes to secure the controls, achieving a crude sort of auto pilot. His arms were then free to loft and swing his Winchester.

Sighting a Taube some 2,000 meters above, he waited until a slow descent signaled the end of the Taube's observation mission; the plane heading back to the German side of the lines. Estimating the Taube's destination, de Brichambaut moved into position to intercept, hoping not to be seen. He positioned the Winchester across his knees and clipped the rubber bands to the stick just as the "Taube, an enormous bird, passed a few (*quelques*) meters above."[10] Swiveling, he fired first at the engine then spaced out his remaining cartridges along the fuselage. The Taube pitched up in a tail stand, recovered, reared up again, and then finally dove to a forced landing on the German side of the lines. Lacking witnesses or confirmation, the French pilot's report was filed away and forgotten.

A second example featured a rescue by a Morane-Saulnier Parasol tractor aircraft, a popular French observation machine designed to be manned by a pilot (Sergeant) in front and observer (Officer) in back. With both aboard, the observer fired the carbine. Developed just before the war, the 1914 sales brochure guaranteed it to climb, with a full military load, to 1,650 feet from sea level in fewer than 6 minutes, all for only 32,000 francs or the then equivalent $5,900.[11] By 1915 the sadly inadequate climb rate would force a reduction in crew size from two to one, but in 1914 optimism still ruled, and with the machine sensed as a bit better than the Henri Farman pusher, a two-man crew was customary for the Parasol.

Late in October 1914, the same hapless Capt. Moris met previously, flying a Henri Farman pusher, a machine similar to that of de Brichambaut,[12] was suddenly caught unawares and attacked by an Albatros shrewdly occupying the Farman's blind side—the machine's rear.[13] As usual Moris was alone, and though equipped with a carbine of his own, was unable to offer return fire, for the engine and propeller blocked access. Evasion seemed his only hope, but the "chicken coop" was well named—it was not a frisky machine.

At this point a Morane-Saulnier Parasol housing pilot Sgt. E. Gilbert and observer Captain de Vergnette hap-

Maurice Farman Shorthorn

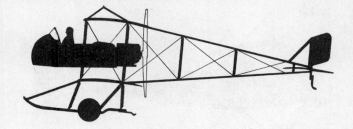

Although hard to visualize as a fighter, the Shorthorn "chicken coop" plus a good carbine added up to a formidable air supremacy weapon in 1914. *Source:* original drawing.

pened along. Gilbert was unusual in having years of experience as a civilian racing pilot.[14] Background mattered: military pilots were skittish over any possibility of collision, while racing pilots accepted the risk of collision as part of the game. Indeed, aggressive positioning within a few feet of the other fellow was a key part of short-course racing.

If Gilbert was unusually well equipped for the job of combat, de Vergnette was not. Rather than risk the one round usually carried in the breech to an uncertain safety, he preferred an empty breech, cutting the ammo supply of his cavalry carbine to a three-round total. Rather than accept the carbine as one more loose nuisance within a small cockpit, he had the gun securely clamped to a main longeron. Of course, given enough time, he could unclamp the gun, chamber a round and swing it aloft—but it would all take time.

Gilbert pulled up to the Albatros and gave de Vergnette time by holding position within the Albatros prop wash. At

Birthing German Army Taubes

Well-regarded Rumpler Taubes in final assembly, 1914. *Source:* photo by Sanke, Berlin, 1914.

Morane-Saulnier Parasol

With its 80 HP engine struggling under a full military load, the Parasol offered a sea level max climb rate of roughly 300 feet per minute—not bad for 1914. *Source:* original drawing.

a range of 22 yards (*vingtaine de metres*) de Vergnette got off his three rounds, permitting Moris to break away and escape from the Albatros. There was more. According to the communique: "The bandit [Albatros] force-landed [on the German side of the lines] in a rough field after an excessive pull-up. It's unlikely that his aircraft can be repaired."[15] One might quibble over any long-range assessment of airworthiness, but by the standards of the time, a "probable" was in order.

How was it done? The key to success in both these incidents was the short range and lack of relative motion between the shooter and target.

If range, speed, and directional differences could be made tiny, then most any kind of gun sight worked well—including no sight at all. The catch was in achieving the necessary extreme closeness and shared direction.

The only practical way to bring it off was to copy Gilbert and home in on the other fellow's prop wash, but few had the ability or the desire. Newly trained RFC pilots arriving at the front with the officially approved "average of 17.5 hours of instruction" could barely fly at all, and even experienced pilots were not up to the task of flying a lightly loaded wing in high turbulence.[16]

Flight training itself painted flight within turbulent air as something to be dreaded. For example, Shorthorn pilot Lt. William Fry noted, "the great thing was to do all flying in as still air as possible and if the wind socks stood out at all from their masts [few chanced it]."[17] Turbulence associated with prop wash was regarded as especially dangerous. Not long before the war, RFC Col. J. E. Capper spoke of employing prop wash as a weapon, "upsetting a hostile craft by giving it one's backwash."[18]

Close pursuit implied flight through enemy prop wash —despite its dubious and even evil reputation. Close pursuit was further damned by the likelihood of collision. Finally, there was the problem of misfires and jammed weapons—leaving the pursuing aggressor clinging to the tail of a thoroughly annoyed tiger. Taking all into account, most pilots were leery of close pursuit and preferred firing from a medium range—say 100 to 300 yards—where gun sights were king.

Infantry sights, lacking the ability to handle a fast-moving crossing target and overly concerned with elevation, clearly wouldn't do. Wanted was some way to assess range and above all to ease the problem of relative motion between target and shooter. Gravity drop or elevation was rated a low priority need, with a built-in average elevation correction—say that for 200 yards—sufficient for any practical purpose.

The first successful air combat sights were of the caliper type, as on the next page. Employed on the Vickers gun bus, a back sight consisting of a rectangular slot, taken together with the usual Lewis bead foresight, did much to assess enemy range and direction.

In detail: the back sight slot was notched, top and bottom, to supply a precise midpoint.[19] Slot width was made equal to the span of the largest likely enemy, when seen at the right range—say the Albatros B1 at 200 yards. Corrections for side views or smaller enemy aircraft were up to the shooter.

A taut wire stretched horizontally across the slot established a base line for elevation. With the enemy machine centered about the wire, the standard 200-yard correction was in effect.

In use, assuming that the enemy crossed to the left, the foresight bead was moved to the extreme left end of the slot; accomplished by swinging the gun to the left, until the hostile machine's nose was placed just touching the bead. For enemy flight to the right, all was reversed. Should the hostile machine be seen head on, the sight was correctly aligned when enemy, bead, and wire were all centered on the slot notches.

These were the simple cases, with instructions that appear practical. However, given more difficult and much likelier encounters, increased judgment was demanded from the shooter. For example, any enemy crossing was unlikely to be of the perfect right-angle type. To deal with an oblique crossing, these were the official instructions

Gun Sights: Vickers FB5 (August 1915)

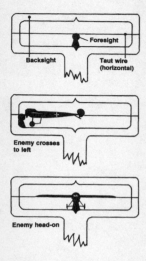

A carefully dimensioned slot was the key to early gun sight accuracy. Source: original drawing. Data input from PRO file #AIR 1/748/204/3/48.

(August 1915): "If the hostile machine is moving diagonally to your left or right, whether away from or towards you, bring the foresight to a position between the center, and the left or right end respectively of the back sight; the closer the hostile enemy approximates to your own course, the closer the foresight should be to the center of the back sight."[20]

Unfortunately for RFC shooters, the advice, when deciphered, was only a cover for the same old Kentucky windage. In shooting at a target moving along an oblique path the devil was in the details, for the precise amount of offset was everything, and to throw the shooter back on his own deficient judgment was to cop out.

The need for something better was shown by the gun sight series employed on the German Fokker E-III, a machine later in time than the Vickers gun bus. The first captured version ('Fokker E-111 Gun Sights,' A, p. 75) employed a concept identical to that of the gun bus, though set up as a foresight, with a pinhole peep sight as back sight. The captors noted that the beads were exactly 43 mm (1.6 in.) on either side of center and "apparently arranged for attacking a machine crossing the front."[21]

The British were not impressed with their gift horse. "It was doubted whether the pilot could use the sight effectively because it was so positioned that he had to raise his head into the propeller slipstream to use it."[22] Nothing was said about the plight of BE2 gunners, required to stand against that same propeller slipstream.

Version B abandoned the adjustable beads in favor of fixed wires; a minor change offering a better-regulated view. Grid sight (C) changed the gun sight role by adding a vertical field of view—here was a design prepared to accept violent changes in altitude.

The favorite form of E-III attack consisted of a dive from altitude, moving downward along an arc behind the victim.[23] Shooting while diving required a sight capable of accepting the victim's anticipated forward motion, much as crossing required anticipation of the victim's lateral motion. The grid sight handled both crossing and diving—one at a time or both simultaneously.

The sight arrangement was prepared for combat ('Using the Grid Sight,' D, p. 76) by adjusting the peep back sight (a tiny hole) until the grid center was on target at some desired range, say 200 yards. Next the shooter reviewed his form of attack (E), to determine the right amount of lead.

At 200 yards, bullets required about ¼ second to arrive at the target. An enemy BE2c might move a full length in this time, but as the attacker moved at an angle relative to his prey, less than a full length of offset was required. With knowledge of the angle of descent and some trigonometry, correct values were calculated. The shooter then memorized all likely descent angles and leads.

The actual view seen in a shooting dive ('Using the Grid Sight,' F, p. 76) was given a circular border, owing to the peep. Because the eye was focused elsewhere—on the target—the border was not sharp. Instead, it seemed a fuzzy circle, with a changeable location established by the position of the shooter's eye. Only when centered, by using the four corners of the grid as markers, was the foresight properly aligned, directing bullets to the grid center. Lead was a matter of offsetting the target relative to the grid center. As shown, this targeted BE2c has been given a lead of about half a length.

The greatest strength and weakness of the device had to do with the peep hole itself.[24] The small hole drilled through an otherwise opaque steel plate had the virtue of forcing visual honesty. The eye was either at the hole or it was blind—there was nothing in between.

With open sight systems, it was possible to be mistaken or to cheat by seeing around the sight, rather than through the sight. British studies using gun cameras found that desperate men shaved a few hundredths of a second off the time required to properly work a sight by seeing around it. In short, the open sight lent itself to self-deluding shooters—the peep did not.

Centering the peep was likely troublesome, but the real catch with peeps was one of the close proximity of the gunner's eye to sight required for operation. Given goggles, a helmet, a great deal of air turbulence and much machine-gun vibration, the necessary steady and close fit of eye to peep was at times impossible to achieve. In contrast, open sights could be worked with the eye a foot or more away. Less demanding, they won out.

Concerning the rectangular grid, critics could argue fairly that no help was given in the case of enemies moving along a diagonal, as seen from the side, diving while crossing. By switching to a system of radial lines, both rectilinear and angled flight paths were accepted.

The resulting combination: ring and post—the name given to open sights with a radial field—defined the next

Fokker E-111 Gun Sights

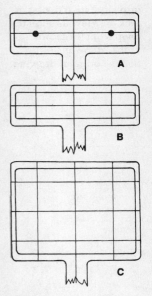

Within the E-III's life span, German gun sights evolved from the bead version (A), to an all wire version (B), and then to the grid sight (C), capable of accepting both crossing and diving targets. *Source:* original drawing. Data input from PRO file #AIR 1/910/204/5/826 and AIR 1/1061/204/5/1579.

Using the Grid Sight

Boresighting (D) at combat range readied the grid sight for a diving attack (E). View through the peep sight (F) shows proper allowance.
Source: original drawing.

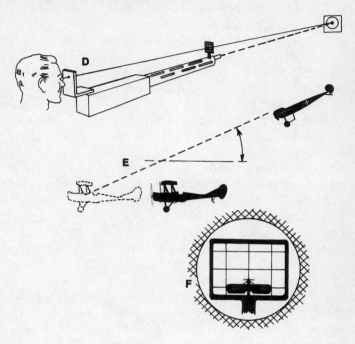

generation of gun sights, a concept adopted in some form by every air service. ("Using the Ring and Post Sight," p.77)

The ring and post concept had the virtues of simplicity and wide application. Aerial gunnery instruction lacked the time to master more complex sighting devices. Here was an easily learned system that suited either fixed or flexible guns. True, it put far too much faith in the inept judgments of poorly trained men, but the demand for fighting men permitted nothing better.

A sense of the aerial gunnery pressures may be gained from a plan originating at the RFC Armament School in July 1918.[25] The idea was to increase the experience level of instructors—not students—to 4 hours 40 minutes of actual shooting time, partly on the ground and partly in the air. Three additional two-seater aircraft were required. The plan was rejected. The reason given: lack of machines. Perhaps this was so, but we are left with a disturbing question: if gunnery instructors were restricted to fewer than 4 hours 40 minutes of shooting experience, how much useful instruction was given to their students? In all likelihood, very

Using the Ring and Post Sight

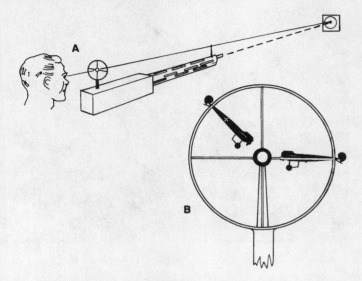

Putting the bead within the inner ring (A) aligned the sight. Range was judged (B) from apparent target size; lead by the distance between bead and target. *Source:* original drawing.

little beyond the usual study of nomenclature and disassembly techniques—useful perhaps, but lacking any connection with shooting. Only by shooting does one learn shooting. As for the many judgments required—range, direction, relative speed—to treat these with quick in-and-out schooling did little to aid newcomer survival.

Old-hand shooters of both fixed and flexible guns learned on their own. A favorite vehicle for self-instruction was the Sopwith Pup, slow and a poor diver, but light, maneuverable, and usually able to evade the more ponderous Albatros. The Pup's single gun was unimpressive compared to the Albatros's two, but regulating one gun was burdensome enough for beginners.

The inevitable disappointment with ring and post sights yielded many design variations. For example, the next generation Sopwith fighter, the two-gun Camel, had an interchanged foresight and back sight, a step taken in the hope of improved accuracy.

A very different concept was fielded by Fokker's D7 and Dr. I Triplane. Here the two guns were given individual small ring sights, each perched on the far end of a Spandau machine gun. Crossed wires divided the field of view and supplied a precise aiming center at the crossover. A small open V/backsight atop each gun completed the arrangement. The overall result was crude, with accuracy limited by gun vibration and tracer gas obscuration.

Sopwith Pup Sights

This Sopwith Pup carried a 5-inch ring sight up front, near the muzzle. The rear sight (right) was of the bead-on-post type. *Source:* original photo, RAFM, Hendon, London, United Kingdom.

However, the crossed wire sights were only low-grade back-up devices. Their use kept the aircraft centerline clear for other sight possibilities, either of the optical lens type or possibly a more elaborate open sight, with a choice to be determined by the pilot. Most chose the optical sight, but Pour-le-Merite fighter pilot Ltn. Karl Thom preferred a Sopwith Pup–type ring sight; big and right up front, immediately behind his D7 radiator.[26] Given a lengthy engine and gun section, the foresight was roughly 8 feet from his eye—a great distance. Gained was a tiny fraction of a second spent refocusing his eye from a far-off enemy to a close-by gun sight; a gain achieved by moving the gun sight toward the enemy. At 8 feet the sight was in sufficiently good focus despite full concentration on the enemy; no back and forth focusing and refocusing was necessary to see both enemy and sight.

A second gain consisted of the realistic field of view offered, much smaller than the usual, a view suggesting the actual bullet strike area, should he fire. In short, there was a case for Thom's form of solution.

In summary:

(1) Gun sight usage required accurate knowledge of enemy range, velocity, and direction. Meager help was offered in making the necessary judgments.

(2) Even with correct input, iron sights could fail owing to improper head location resulting from turbulence, gun vibration, or impatience.

Chapter 4

Sopwith Camel Sights

With the Camel, Sopwith changed its mind and put the ring sight close to the pilot. What seems a model airplane engine (left) was a windmill and compressor serving to pressurize the fuel tank. *Source:* original photo, RAFM, Hendon, London, United Kingdom.

Extra Sights

The Fokker D7 crossed wire sights, one per gun, offered the extra sight as a backup. A third, more sophisticated sight, was sometimes carried as well. *Source:* original photo, Musee de L'Air, Paris, France.

(3) Most iron sights required endless changes of eye focus from target to gun sight and back again, slowing the targeting process.

Although similar attempts to rework single-seater iron sights continued throughout the war, most such variations were minor, amounting to little more than custom fitting. The one startling change in technology came from a complex optical device—the Aldis sight. The Aldis and its Ger-

One Pleased User

With gun sight drawbacks only too obvious, the beaming satisfaction of this SPAD 13 pilot owed more to propaganda than reality. *Source:* USAAF Training Command, *Fighter Gunnery* (Washington, D.C.: USGPO, 1944), 12.

man counterpart came to play an important role in the late war period, when stock SE5a's and many Fokker Triplanes were supplied with the device.

What hope was there for fancy optics within air so often stuffed with freezing mist? Why sight through glass smeared with flying oil droplets?

5

Advanced Gunnery

ALTHOUGH IT HAD THE APPEARANCE OF a telescope and was usually referred to as a telescopic sight, the Aldis neither enlarged nor reduced the viewed scene.

The view was exactly the same, through the Aldis or not.[1] So much so that one eye could be held to the sight and the other left open, facing the same view, and all without confusion. One major sighting advantage over ordinary open sights was offered: a tolerance for sizable errors in eye location.

Even large eye position errors were acceptable without penalty (as in "Using the Aldis Sight," p. 83, C). The same

Pilot's View, Camel Cockpit

Located on center between the twin Vickers (capped with crash buffers) is an Aldis sight, immediately under a backup ring sight. *Source:* Australian War Memorial, negative #E04899. Unit: Squadron #4, Australian Flying Corps.

positioning error—say half an inch off center—would lead to complete blockage or blindness with a peep sight, and to many yards of misjudged error with an open sight. All was well, and the sight free from error, so long as the entire inner (small) circle could be seen.

Otherwise, sighting problems remained much the same. Relative speed, closing angle, and yaw determination were the shooter's problem, as before, for in these areas the Aldis offered nothing more than open sights. Once again, range estimation employed wingspan as a yardstick, with the outer circle diameter usually set equal to the span of the Albatros fighter series.

There were some small pluses and nice touches. For example, options included ('Using the Aldis Sight,' B, p. 82–83) a choice of engraved glass discs, each speed rated with an inner ring offering a suggested lead offset. When the enemy nose touched the ring, one fired. Neat—if the enemy speed matched that number stamped on the glass, and if his path was really at a right angle to the shooter, and if the assessed range was as judged. The likelihood of all being correct was small. Many adjustments were required for compensation. Yet shooters had little notion of the "clicks" required and the pace of combat allowed no time for reflection. In the end, much was luck and Kentucky windage. In this mean world, small pluses counted for little. The success of the unadorned crossed axes disc (A) was understandable; here was a vote against nice touches—and self-deception.

As for price, there were three special Aldis drawbacks: (a) the device couldn't be used under low light conditions, (b) it wasn't suited for flexible gun use, and (c) the optical system was subject to misting over by oil droplets landing on the exposed glass face.[2]

Of these (c) was the most important, and with many British pilots flying behind rotary engines notorious for flinging oil, reason enough for pilots to insist upon an open sight back-up for their Aldis. German pilots too had their reservations. Ace Maj. K. Degelow went so far as to condemn the entire telescopic sight concept as falsely based.[3] As he saw matters, wanted was a close approach to the enemy, not a better gun sight, for no gun sight could supply the huge increase in shooting accuracy achieved through close approach. As for the goal of fighting at a remote, collision-free distance, courtesy of better gun sights, he considered the prospect to be so much nonsense.

Whatever their doubts, pilots came to accept the Aldis

Using the Aldis Sight

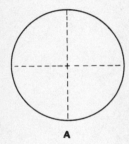

A

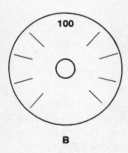

B

Aldis optional etched backgrounds included simple crossed axes (A) or a set of radial lines (B) with an inner circle offering the right amount of lead for a crossing enemy at the indicated speed. →

The Aldis Survives

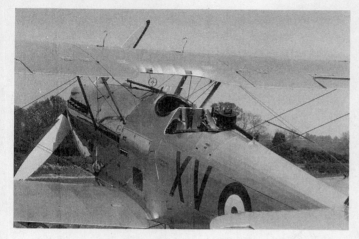

A paired open sight and Aldis (long black tube) continued as first line fighting tools for a generation. Shown: Hawker Hart, circa 1935. *Source:* original photo, air show, Biggleswade, United Kingdom.

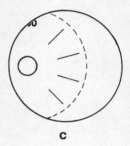

C

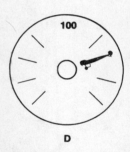

D

as a useful accessory. Alone, it was a bit too sensitive, but paired with an open sight the combination served well as an all-purpose, all-weather gun sight, managing to soldier on for a generation.

With widespread acceptance came the inevitable misuse. In September 1917, British RFC Intelligence struggled with the problem of Gotha markings. The giant bomber was listed as carrying unusually small markings—an odd German move given the great expanse of canvas available for display. Shortage of paint?

The answer came out of the Aldis used to sight the bombers.[4] Set to the usual standard—an Albatros fighter wingspan—the sight required an enormous range to accept the Gotha's huge span. To the British pilot cruising about at 500 yards, sniffing out the Gotha, the "Iron Cross" markings appeared "about twice as small"—a reflection of increased range, not decreased size. The analyst assigned the problem knew something about scale effect, and so the small markings case was solved. The pilot was not commended.

Employment of the Aldis concept helped the fighting pilot, but did nothing for the gunner/observer working a flexible gun. On test, the Aldis flexible mount proved heavy and clumsy and interfered with the changing of Lewis drums.[5] With the Aldis possibility dead, improved flexible gun sight hopes focused on the flexible gunner's basic problem—allowing for his own aircraft's speed.

Not only did flexible gunners have every aiming prob-

(Using the Aldis Sight, cont.)

In use, even a large error in centering the eye (C) produced no alignment error–here was the main advantage. Range assessment (D) was based on the outer circle diameter equaling enemy wingspan when at the correct range. Case shown: enemy too far; move closer. *Source:* original drawing; input, chapter 5, note 1.

Using the Vane Sight

Bullets fired laterally (A) were carried forward by aircraft motion, preventing aiming accuracy. Using the relative wind to drive a bead foresight by means of vanes (B) angled the shooter's line of sight forward, offering compensation. *Source:* original drawing.

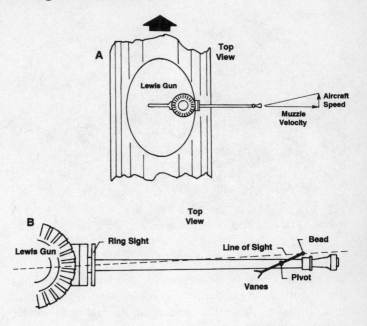

lem of the fixed gunner, but one more besides—bullet displacement owing to the shooter's motion through the air. All bullets, whether from fixed or flexible guns, were given a forward push by the shooter's aircraft motion. In the case of fixed guns, the usual firing direction was straight ahead, and the small amount of aircraft speed compared to muzzle velocity—about 6 percent—produced a negligible change in aim. However, a flexible gun firing directly left or right sensed that same 6 percent as a shift in aim amounting to roughly an aircraft length and a half at 200 yards. If ignored, this amounted to a large error, preventing accuracy.

Wanted was a device that would cut in or out as needed while the gunner moved his Lewis about, becoming fully effective when the gun was pointed due left or right, or at right angles to the aircraft direction, and yet fading to inaction as the line of fire moved toward the aircraft front or rear. The vane sight and especially the Norman vane sight was the area's major British development.[6] Our sketches offer a sense of concept, though not of complexity, for all means of adjustment—and there were many— have been eliminated in the interest of clarity.

The core idea was a continuously shifting foresight bead, repositioning itself automatically as the gun moved

Vane Sight Details

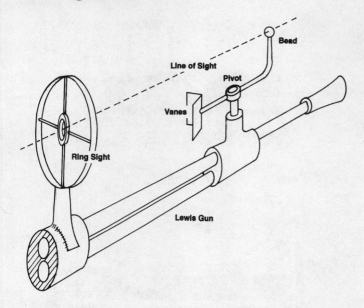

With a weathervane-like action, the twin vanes pushed the bead sight against prevailing crosswinds. For head-on or following winds, there was no bead displacement. *Source:* original drawing.

about. To drive the bead, use was made of the wind surrounding the gun to press against a set of vanes in weathervane fashion. With the gun directly across the wind, wind push was a maximum, shoving the bead into the wind and bringing the line of fire a bit forward—through that important 6 angular degrees of correction. Moving the gun axis away from a perfect crosswind location eased the push force; the bead swinging toward a zero correction position, finally attained when the gun axis pointed directly upwind or downwind.

Did it work? Not very well. However, a sense of overwhelming burden led to great patience in evaluating flexible gun sights—criticism was easy, but where was the alternative? The Norman worked well enough to tantalize users, and to maintain its approved status, despite obvious defects.

Of these, the greatest was sensitivity to local turbulence about the gunner's cockpit—everything from wing downwash, to spiraling prop wash, to separated flow streaming from windscreens, and so forth, influenced the vanes. These unwanted winds had little to do with bullet path, but the vanes responded to any and all airflow, whether pertinent or not.

In practice, complaints of large Norman errors resulted

Location determined accuracy of the Norman sight. *Source:* original drawing.

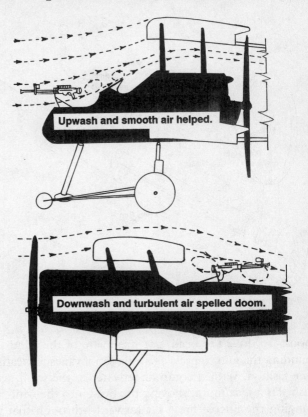

Upwash and smooth air helped.

Downwash and turbulent air spelled doom.

in orders to raise the aim of all Lewis guns equipped with the sight by some 8½ feet, when at 300 yards range.[7] The timing of the order (April 30, 1917) at the very end of Bloody April, implied that no effective defense was available for two-seater gunners caught up in the period's murderous German attacks. True, 300 yards was beyond the normal fighting distance, and a shorter, practical range would experience fewer than an 8½ feet drop. However, even a 4-foot drop was serious, and the Norman suffered a large horizontal shift as well, with partial results suggesting a 4-foot left or right error, also at 300 yards. The official conclusion: "The Norman windvane affords at best only a very rough compensation sight, suitable enough for the rough and tumble of short-range fighting of 1917, but not sufficiently accurate for longer-range work . . . every effort should therefore be made to replace it." The greatest errors came about in firing directly backward, a firing position "more often required than any other," for this was the

Competition for the Norman

Vane type sights competed with a geared correction system based on a circular turret. German LVG CVI shown. *Source:* original photo, air show, Biggleswade, United Kingdom.

basic defensive shooting position of a two-seater under attack by a single-seater. Here the vane sight was found "inaccurate and unsteady"—likely the result of a vane position located in the wind shadow of the shooter—a zone of unsteady separated airflow; backflow, and powerful eddies ruled by turbulence.[8]

Far from appreciating the new Norman instructions, sour protests poured in from the field. Pusher aircraft equipped with vane sights, for example the FE2d, were then declared exempt from the change order. In some strange fashion, officials decided, pusher "wind vane errors are different [from tractors] and apparently neutralize the other errors." For those able to follow the confused instructions, the final result was a "grouping of the shots fired . . . when the gun is being traversed and firing continuously of rarely, if ever, less than 20 ft. in diameter at 300 yards."[9]

Forced to accept so large a bullet scatter, shooters turned cynical—what difference did a typical Norman's aiming correction of a few feet make, when bullet scatter was many times as bad? Perhaps only corrections of "six feet or more are worth allowing for" ran one comment from the field, with much logic on its side.[10]

Despite the criticism, the vane sight soldiered on. For

Gear-Driven Gun Sight

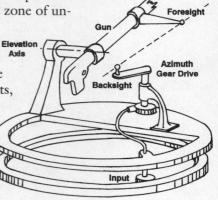

Gears converted left-right and fore-aft gun locations into the proper amount of back sight offset. *Source:* original drawing much influenced by Pugachev, *Teoria Vozdushnoi Strel*, 49.

lateral firing, it was better than no device at all likely ranges, and fairly accurate at a close range, say 100 yards. As for a next generation replacement, only one possibility was known—a moving gun sight offering automatic compensation by means of a tricky gear arrangement. After an early look, the British opted for the simpler vane solution, leaving the gear concept to the Germans.

In operation, geared gun sight correction required the shooter to haul his gun around a special cockpit, built around a perfect circle. Geared to the circle was a flexible shaft and follower gear, converting the gun's angular position into a corresponding adjustment of the gun's back sight—usually a bead. The gearing was chosen to yield zero correction with the gun located either fore or aft, and offered maximum compensation for either left or right gun positioning. Those in-between attitudes were granted just the right amount of back sight offset. All things considered, the compensation scheme was far more certain than the vane drive because cockpit turbulence couldn't influence the outcome. Gun elevation was not regulated or impeded in any way.

Drawbacks started with the cost and complexity of the system. Next came the unnatural turret motion forced on the shooter. Most shooters wanted the freedom of a bird hunter; that is, the right to swing a weapon as desired. Instead, the turret forced him to accept many built-in constraints. To shoot left, he moved the turret left. Fair enough, but he had no fine-tuning option. His gun swung about a large fixed radius reflecting the turret design, and the instant sensitivity of a freely pivoting mount was gone. Finally, the moving apparatus added much mass and inertia to that of the gun. With only limited human strength available as driving power, the result was a sluggish response at an exhausting cost, especially so at high altitude in a pre-oxygen time.

Choosing between the error-prone vane system or the correct but burdensome gear drive system was not a simple matter. The British chose simplicity and least encumbrance, albeit with low accuracy.[11] As British gunnery expert and ace Maj. Lenoe Hawker saw it: "the turret . . . has two disadvantages—slow to traverse and firing up[wards] is difficult."[12] In opting for greater accuracy, the Germans paid a stiff price in reduced shooting deftness.

Searches for the lesser evil revolve about negative, disturbing factors. In this case, there were two additional headaches acting to throw doubt on all flexible gun sights—the problem of maneuvering, and secondly, gun sight inability to cope with circular trajectory.

In combat, gunners had little control or foreknowledge of violent maneuvers entered by their pilots. The unhappy effect of such maneuvers was to add a component of aircraft maneuvering velocity to the gunner's departing bullets, in much the same manner as the lateral shooting case, considered above. However, unlike lateral error, maneuverability error could be experienced in most any direction, with a strength depending partly on the maneuver and partly on the fierceness and anxiety gripping the pilot. There was no way of compensating for the resulting erratic bullet path. Officialdom's advice—not to shoot when the aircraft was bucking, sliding, or yawing—smacked of "let them eat cake" evasion.[13] For the truly desperate, there were times when shooting was the only hope. To do without shooting while maneuvering was a most serious constraint.

The natural result was to raise doubts about sights—all flexible gun sights—and to bring into question those gains in accuracy produced by vanes or turrets. If fancy sights couldn't deliver shooting accuracy while maneuvering, why bother? Why not stick to simple sights?

The second problem—circular trajectory—raised further doubts. Consider two opposing two-seaters circling each other at a large but still practical shooting range, say 300 yards. Each machine flies a perfect banked circle at a steady speed, so that holding the other fellow within one's sights is easy. Indeed, the enemy aircraft appears stationary in the sights. The air is clear and still. How much lead is to be used?

Both gunners have been taught that the rate at which open sights are crossed by an enemy machine reflects crossing speed. The greater the speed, the more lead is required. One gunner reasons that as the target never moves within his sights, no lead is necessary, and all that he need do is center the target and shoot. The opposing gunner decides that something is wrong—obviously his enemy's speed isn't zero. Disgusted, he decides that the apparently stationary target means that his sights are worthless. In despair, he applies an arbitrary lead of many whole aircraft lengths—an extraordinary amount, well beyond anything he can fit into his sights. Which gunner was more likely to be correct?

The despairing skeptic was much more likely to be right. If both gunners had simple open sights and fired

Shooting across a Circle

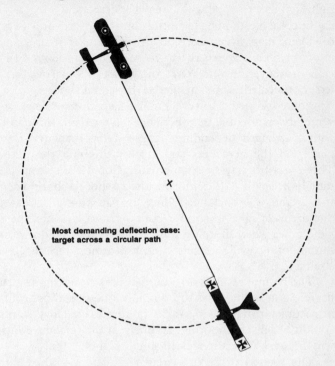

**Most demanding deflection case:
target across a circular path**

across a distance of 300 yards, the no-lead shooter's bullets
would fall behind his target by several aircraft lengths.
Only a great deal of lead could save the situation.

In reality, the circling case came up often enough and
was recognized by the establishment as potentially profitable—but gunners were on their own. Sometimes sights
could be used to judge enemy airspeed and sometimes
not—it was all a matter of flight path, where straight lent
itself to sights and curved did not. As combat moved back
and forth between the two, choice and implementation
was the gunner's problem.

Should a gunner's lot seem especially hard, the injunc-
tion against maneuvering also covered an important fixed
gun case: yaw was frowned upon when shooting. In lining
up on an enemy, it was perfectly natural to achieve a last
moment left-right correction by pressing on the rudder
pedals, turning the nose slightly in the desired direction.
Doing so without bank in a low dihedral machine produced yaw, a slipping, skidding motion through the air, as
the machine continued to head in the old direction despite
the fresh orientation. In effect, the machine was flying
slightly sideways. Firing meant that each bullet emerged

Single Flexible Gun for Maneuverability

Standard F2b Bristol Fighter rear gun consisted of a single Lewis gun on a Scarff mount—easily handled but low in bullet density. *Source:* original photos, (top) air show, Biggleswade, United Kingdom; (bottom) RAFM, Hendon, London, United Kingdom.

with a sideways push—exactly the same situation existent in lateral firing—although the usual amount of last-second aiming yaw supplied a much smaller error. Even so, it was easily possible to mistakenly shift the bullet strike area by 5 feet at 300 yards; a matter of losing accuracy by seeking it at the last moment.

Given the simpler problem of shooting straight ahead, single-seater pilots soon learned to prefer two guns. They correctly saw two gun odds as better—though not twice as good—for two guns aimed in the wrong direction were no better than one. Still, all things considered, two fixed guns were better. What of flexible guns?

Flexible gunners had special problems. Their shooting accuracy was made worse by the lateral aiming uncertainty,

Two Guns for Bullet Density

Two guns meant twice as many bullets, but the rig weight and high G positioning difficulties prevented enthusiasm. *Source:* Australian War Memorial; negative #B02040.

a factor tending to push two guns as a solution. However, even a single loaded Lewis gun with mount weighed in at well over 32 pounds. Shoving two of these about in a precise pattern required enormous strength, especially so when bucking high-G maneuvers at upper altitudes. The relative ease of handling one gun, versus the physical demands of two, made for a difficult trade-off. The two-seater Bristol Fighter (F2b) offered a choice.

The basic Scarff mount offered a rough weight balance, obtained by pivoting the gun mass close to its center of gravity, and employing shock cord as a form of counterbalance. It worked well enough with one gun. However, hard-pressed gunners were unable to cope with two guns when experiencing the 3Gs rising out of violent maneuvering. The necessary degree of balance wasn't there—too much depended on brute strength. Gunner disappointment was reflected in the official RAF summing up: "Nine out of ten of the experienced Bristol Fighter gunners preferred a single gun."[14]

Yet there was a role for two gun rear turrets. Much depended on the aircraft. The F2b was employed largely as an aggressive interceptor, and used those violent maneuvers common to the breed. Other machines, especially underpowered aircraft serving as cooperation aircraft or light bombers, led relatively passive lives. It was precisely these aircraft that needed a strong defense, for their very lack of maneuverability drew enemy attackers.

Gunner's Choice

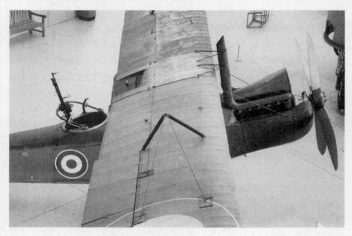

RE8 rear gunners were supplied with either one Lewis gun (top, left) or two guns (bottom, right). In addition, pilots had their own side-mounted Vickers. Note Aldis sight. Sources: (top) photo: www.geocities.com/ aerodromeaces; (bottom) original photo, IWM, Duxford, U.K.

The RE8 was such a machine. Powered with an engine offering 140 HP at a time when most opposing single-seaters had more than 200 HP available, it required gifted gunnery to survive one-on-one combat.

At times a kind of spoofing served better than gunnery, for unlike the F2b, the RE8 was concerned largely with survival and not with combat. One way to survive was to overawe the opposition—to put up a display of fireworks discouraging to all but the most intrepid of pursuers. Twin guns firing a high percent of tracers was a good fit. As given by Lt. W. B. Farrington "[twin gun] mass impeded movement, especially from side to side," but offered "a double volume of fire, a spare gun, and considerable moral effect upon the enemy."[15]

For the F2b, employed to win within the world of real combat, fireworks displays were nonsense and the second Lewis was unwanted. In the case of the sluggish RE8, the gain in moral effect may well have been worth 32 pounds weight. In short, the airplane and its purpose had much to do with the profit, if any, bought by a second Lewis. This very dependency on precise circumstances suggested only small potential gains. Unhappily, given poor rear gunner shooting accuracy, even doubling the number of bullets changed little.

Why was his accuracy so low? To sum up: in addition to the excessive physical demands placed on the rear gunner by prop blast and maneuvering accelerations, there was the matter of recoil forces not fully countered, of necessary clearance between moving parts of a flimsy tubular gun mount, and an inability to cope with lateral shooting when uncertain both of his own speed and that of his enemy. Which was the major villain?

To find out, Orfordness tested an RE8 with a single rear gun.[16] Again, the target was a large flag, lofted by a balloon. To undercut cumulative recoil effects, only one round was fired per attack. To eliminate sight errors, many trial runs were permitted, with the sights corrected as required. In time, the gunner knew the range, azimuth, and aircraft heading by heart: 250 yards, aircraft speed roughly 90 MPH, azimuth 30 degrees abaft the beam. On a day of light winds, the RE8 simulated eight attack runs. The average error (mean divergence) from the center of hits was measured to be 5 feet—and this after sight corrections amounting to 5 feet in the direction of flight and 2 feet vertically.

Orfordness announced their satisfaction, for shooting "within 5 or 6 ft. at 250 yards [is] an accuracy quite sufficient for purposes of general aircraft gunnery."[17] Possibly, but noting the too ideal test circumstances, introduction of more realistic conditions would have expanded the mean center of hit error plus scatter limits to a less desirable figure—all the way to that enormous 45-foot circle realized on a bumpy day, noted previously.

Yet the test had value in demonstrating the multiplicity of villains. Everything counted. Although the pilot was doing his best, aircraft speed was not perfectly regulated and could be off by 2 MPH. Wind speed itself was beyond control: "light" meant any velocity below 10 MPH. Adding these errors, speed over the ground could be out by 13 percent. Range estimation involved similar uncertain judgments and errors. In short, each supposedly fixed quantity was actually somewhat vague. Inevitably, the combination of multiple errors produced markedly different bullet trajectories. In short, the judgment required was so fine that only an expert flexible gunner, after many practice sessions, could hope to place the center of his bullets at 5 feet from the bull's-eye, when at 250 yards range on a calm day. Under more realistic conditions, little hope existed for the average gunner.

The same basic difficulties existed in fixed gunnery. Lengthy training was required to achieve even a mediocre level of skill, and as noted by ace Squadron Leader Leonard H. Rochford, the authorities were reluctant to grant even minimal instruction. As evidence, he offered the records of two fighter pilots serving with him, neither of whom had fired a single round in the air prior to arrival at the front (1918).[18] Including Rochford, the totally unprepared pilots numbered three—admittedly a small number, but a significant portion of his squadron.

These three did learn the necessary skill on their own, for no matter what the odds, some will survive. However, Rochford's on-the-job training was seriously incomplete. Analyzing his own combat claims, he found, "About two-thirds [of the encounters] produced no definite result. Several other pilots of our squadron, all with good fighting records, confirmed this ratio as about correct."[19]

His conclusion: they still couldn't shoot. Shooting was difficult and a literally hit-or-miss form of on-the-job training was not the way to learn. Why was management so stingy with instruction? More than wartime confusion was involved. RFC plans minimized all instruction—flying and shooting—in part fearing delay in the supply of fresh fighting men at the front, in part concerned over wastage losses in instruction, and in part over doubts concerning the amount of profit to be found through instruction.

Prewar thinking concerning air-fighting losses suggested a low number, consistent with the belief that reconnaissance was the proper role for aircraft, and aerial fighting a rare and largely pointless affair. Schools were established to supply the low estimated demand for fresh pilots. When real world events of 1915 showed this view to be wrong, the RFC refused to be stampeded and moved carefully to

The classic painting of George H. Davis (1919) shows a group of DH9's tightening formation under attack. Every rear gunner responds. *Source:* original photo, painting displayed IWM, London, United Kingdom.

change matters. More students meant more instructors and these were obtained at a bargain price by shunting available old hands into the job. Unfortunately, many were combat-fatigued types, happy to get away from battle, but riven by fear of flying. These men made terrible instructors, at times refusing to let students touch the controls for fear of a fatal mistake.[20] Brig. Gen. Sefton Brancker, in charge of filling the pipeline to the front, and also chief of instruction, admitted publicly (January 1917), "I suppose only about 10% of our flying officers are really good instructors."[21] Rather than eliminate rotten instruction, management opted for a more pleasing idea: instruction was largely a waste of effort. Those who had the knack would learn on their own. Those who didn't were lost anyway.

Backing this conclusion were the casualty records of those in training, amounting to one fatal casualty per 1,170 training hours.[22] Put another way, if 1,170 students were set the task of aerial instruction, crashes would abound. One student would die each hour of the day. Many more would be seriously injured per hour, and invalided out of the service. Hundreds of mechanics would be tied up in making repairs and tuning up trainers.

Flexible Gun Accuracy Test

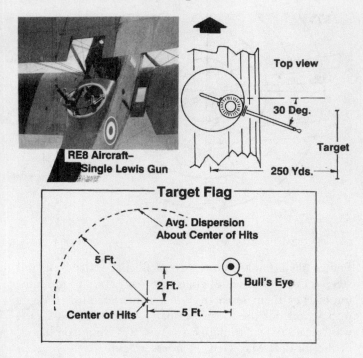

Top view

30 Deg.

Target

250 Yds.

RE8 Aircraft–
Single Lewis Gun

Target Flag

Avg. Dispersion
About Center of Hits

5 Ft.

2 Ft.

Bull's Eye

Center of Hits — 5 Ft.

At 250 yards, tests showed an average scatter of 5 feet about a hit center located more than 5 feet from the bull's-eye. Under combat shooting conditions, the anticipated error was much greater. Sources: original photo, IWM, Duxford, United Kingdom; original drawings, with data input Orfordness final report, p. 30.

To sense training difficulties, consider a favored gunnery exercise consisting of diving to shoot at a small pond. With bullet splashes registering hits, the process was cheap, required no maintenance, and offered much learning. However, as pointed out by Lt. William Bishop, when given a realistically sized target, "You have to dive steeply at this and there is very little margin of safety when plunging at full speed to within a few feet of the earth."[23]

Even skilled fighter pilots didn't regard such a plunge as routine. For tyro pilots, it was an invitation to disaster.

A relatively safe method of instruction featuring the use of a gun camera instead of bullets lent itself to mock combat and so had great appeal. The catch was one of the considerable degree of sophistication required to interpret results. A photo of the line of fire was all very well, but determination of the strike point required correction for the bullet's time of flight, the yaw of the attacking aircraft, and finally the speed, attitude, and direction of the target. Such corrections called for flair and experience, qualities frequently lacking in RFC instruction.

Brancker, always struggling to keep his pipeline to

Scoring Gun Camera Photos

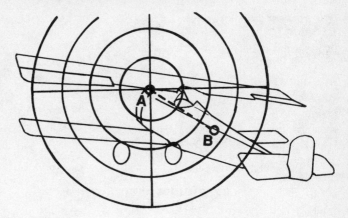

Photos showing aiming point (A) were analyzed to determine strike point (B). Much judgment was required. Decision, this case: near miss pilot; not enough lead. *Source: original drawing suggested by data of Vaughan, ed., American Pilot in the Skies of France, 92.*

France filled, saw the answer to ineffective instruction and steep training losses as obvious: cut instruction to the minimum. Let them learn over the front. Sending students into action, for the most part barely able to fly or shoot, was certain to lead to high casualties. RFC high command, in the form of Maj. Gen. Henderson, anticipated such an outcome for the good reason: "RFC pilots, except those who had been flying on the Western Front for some time, were by comparison [to the Germans] inexperienced."[24]

The upshot was an average service life measured in months in the summer of 1917, amounting to four months for gunners and two and a half months for single-seater pilots.[25] By including a few casualties of the wily old-timer type, the averaging process tended to hide the real victims: ignorant newcomers lacking the skills necessary to survive, shot dead within a few weeks of arriving at the front.

We now believe that each soldier is precious and that every effort must be made to equip fighting men with essential skills. To grant newcomer fighter pilots "at least 15 hours in the air solo" (March 1916), or 17 hours (August 1917) along with some limited firing of weapons, now seems murderously inadequate.[26] The Great War period reflected very different values.

Henderson, Brancker, and Trenchard were not chairborne brass hats. Each was a pilot. Trenchard had served as an instructor and then as a chief of instructors. Henderson was a degreed engineer with an officer son serving the RFC in France. These were bright, active, responsible administrators, well aware of frontline operational problems. True, their solution to the pipeline problem was not ours, but the "lions led by donkeys" type of bitter criticism must be dismissed as grotesque.[27] These particular lions were led by lions.

Although the RFC/RAF leaders lacked genius, neither were they fools. They struggled to win on their terms, believing in the poorly prepared many, as against the gifted, highly trained few. In the end, British air fighting strategy was exonerated, for the many won. The catch was in the cost. Especially painful were those men lost owing to ignorance, to unfamiliarity with their tools.

To the game fighter pilot or gunner, mulling over his own shooting inadequacy, there was only one practical answer—get closer. All shooting errors increased steadily with range. As the French carbine shooters had discovered, when at point blank range, all sighting problems disappeared—it wasn't necessary to allow for gravity, relative velocity, flight path, or range. Once at 20 yards distance, everybody was a crack shot.

This left only one problem—attaining that magic position. One needed the right aircraft, one with a superior performance not easily obtained from low power Allied engines. As openly admitted by Henderson (January 1918): "We were at a disadvantage because our planes were underengined."[28] How then was a point blank shooting position achieved?

One practical technique employed a pull-down gun, used directly under an enemy aircraft. To get into the right position with a low power aircraft, the gunner/observer position was eliminated. The weight saved yielded a bit more performance, just enough for a skilled pilot employing stealth to sneak into the right position. Once there, the gun was pulled down and the enemy overhead blasted. The attractive simplicity of the scheme alone attracted users, and this one had a special cachet—aces Lt. Albert Ball and Lt. Billy Bishop had made it their specialty, achieving much success in the process. For a time, it worked well indeed.

First broad usage came with the Nieuport 11, a lightweight French biplane mounting a single Lewis above the upper wing, set to shoot over the propeller. Design features included the ability to shoot at a steep upward angle or straight ahead, as desired; the absence of a synchronizer with its sometimes suicidal malfunctions; and better visibility over the unadorned cowling. Drawbacks were those of

The French Solution

The Nieuport's wing-top Lewis gun and its two controlling lanyards. Pulling the left cable brought the gun closer to the pilot. Pulling the right cable fired the gun. *Source:* original photo, Musee de L'Air, Paris, France.

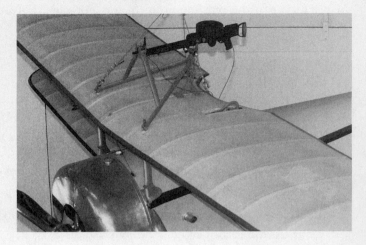

remote reloading, and the even greater problem of clearing cartridge jams at a distance.

In use, two lanyards were supplied the pilot. Pulling the first unlatched a snap lock at the muzzle end of the gun. Once free, both air drag and weight acted to pivot the gun, automatically moving the Lewis spade handle toward the pilot's head. He could now hope to reach upward and change drums or clear a cartridge. However, most men found it necessary to stand up to work effectively—accepting the strong prop wash currents—all while flying the machine. It was a most demanding process.

Once reloaded or cleared of a jam, the pilot swung the gun butt upward sharply, slamming the muzzle home on its bipod support and latching the gun securely. So primitive an operating system would seem to be fail-proof. Yet there were difficulties. Some were aerodynamic, for drums hit by powerful air blasts fell from numbed fingers, striking or lodging in the controls. Other problems resulted from inherent Lewis limitations.

Firing in the approved style of five rounds per burst required replacement of the standard, smaller-sized drum, before ten bursts were expended. Common sense pushed for replacement remote from combat, in some quiet corner of the sky, by breaking off long before all forty-seven rounds were fired. In contrast, opposing German single-seaters were in a position to calmly hose away two hundred rounds without concern over supply. Fear of running out of bullets resulted in a miserly expenditure, with some

Bishop Demonstrates Upward Firing

His Nieuport 17 replaced the 11's simple pivot with a short slide, but the basic concept was unchanged: get close and shoot from the enemy blind spot! *Source:* www.geocities.com/ TimesSquare/Zone/ 4914/images/bishlewis.

opportunities passed up. In effect, all Lewis gun-equipped pilots carried an extra, bookkeeping burden.

While all observer/gunners faced similar reloading problems, pilots were expected to fly the aircraft and plot tactics while reloading. Special gun-tending demands placed upon its one-man crew by the Nieuport 11, 17, and SE5a did much to lessen enthusiasm for the remote gun notion.

Yet, the remote-gunned, maneuverable fighter could work well indeed. For example, despite its tiny engine, the 80 HP Nieuport 11 did much to choke off the Fokker E-III menace. Forward looking French Air Service members saw to its redesign, improving weak points. The same one-gun concept was made a bit handier, and the resulting package given more power, to emerge as the highly successful Nieuport 17, able to shoot straight ahead, straight up, or anywhere in between.

Stealth and surprise were key components of the concept. To approach closely was usually impossible if given a loud and clear arrival at the scene of battle. Much depended on lurking about and catching the other fellow unawares.

Capt. James B. McCudden owed much to a skilled, sneaky approach to his target. Working alone, he made shrewd use of the heavy workload given to German

"The Sitter"

observers. Once at high altitude, struggling with the demands of a precisely timed photographic series, observers paid little attention to whatever was immediately beneath them. Their blindness was reinforced by pilots unable to see to the rear. As a result, in December 1917, "I shot down 6 two-seaters in succession without any enemy aircraft getting a single shot at me."[29] Here was craftiness of a high order.

Lt. Albert Ball developed a different tactic. Usually alone, he headed for large enemy formations to launch his unique form of solo attack. Interestingly, the steep odds against him seemed to work in his favor, for the German formations usually broke up, with machines getting in one another's way as they desperately avoided collision. Thriving on the confusion and firing his pull-down gun at negligible ranges, Ball ran up a large score quickly. The extreme maneuverability of the Nieuport 17 was essential to his point blank style—one of catch-as-catch-can combat.

He wasn't keen on the SE5a. The relatively sedate, though powerful SE didn't stress maneuverability, though most found it adequate. Instead, speed was offered—a pointless virtue in the Ball scheme of things. To McCudden, the SE5a's plentiful power at extreme altitude was important. Within the limits of his own eccentric fighting mode, he was an enthusiast.

In general, pilots liked the SE5a but thought poorly of the remote Lewis gun. Two independently triggered Vickers, close by, seemed a better bet. As for the upward shooting possibility, the SE5a had enough excess power to permit a strong zoom with some shooting at the peak, before breaking off to stall. True, this was not easy to bring off; yet in expert hands it was a workable concept, without the drawbacks of a remote gun.

What was wrong with the pull-down gun? An official survey of four squadrons (December 1917) turned up these objections:

1. Necessity of changing drums—a constant source of worry to pilots in a fight.
2. Difficulty of changing drums on unstable machines [i.e., Nieuport, Camel].
3. Extreme difficulty in correcting jams.
4. In cold weather the gun [Lewis] freezes up more readily than the Vickers owing to its exposed position.
5. Additional head resistance, lowering performance.
6. Very much more satisfactory having [only] one type gun in Squadron [simplifying repairs].
7. Since [improvements] to the Vickers guns, the rapid fire advantage which the Lewis formerly had, has been done away with.[30]

The list was damning. To many pilots, the crucial pull-down drawback was the reduction of performance owing to extra drag. Limited use, largely restricted to fighting enemy two-seaters, was another major factor. With Ball's death, and McCudden's assignment to England (February 1918), the pull-down gun, already under wide attack, lost crucial support. If not quite "abandoned" by March 1918, it held few believers.[31]

One last reason for disillusionment had to do with the Gotha tunnel: a means of eliminating two-seater blind spots, permitting the rear gunner to shoot downward and backward. The tardy arrival of so obvious a solution testified to a formidable design problem, for it was necessary to eliminate many fuselage cross braces in order to clear a line

Even with the gun located remotely, the Nieuport's visibility was poor. Note the Aldis sight. Source: original photo, Canadian War Museum, Ottawa, Canada.

of fire. Redesign required flair to avoid a weak and willowy shell.

The Gotha 10 employed a long plywood arch as a substitute structure, with bullets passing through a hole in the top deck and under the open lower side of the arch. Guide rails permitted lateral gun travel. The Parabellum machine gun, Germany's equivalent of the Lewis, could either be depressed to fire through a long, semielliptical hole, or elevated to fire in the standard fashion.

It was an ingenious solution; one that would evolve into World War II's tail gun. The very determination of attackers to approach closely and fly at a matching speed, eliminating deflection and sighting problems, made matters that much simpler for Gotha 10 gunners. Their targets seemed neatly suspended at the far end of the tunnel, inviting destruction.

In sum, intensive gunnery development efforts did result in slight improved accuracy through better sights—optical, geared, and vane. Twin gun experience showed a greater frequency of hits, when used as fixed guns, but

Bishop's Gun Arrangement

View looking forward from the rudder. Of all instruments, only the vital airspeed indicator was placed on top of the cowling. The gun was within reach—but not easy reach. *Source:* original photo, Canadian War Museum, Ottawa, Canada.

Gotha Surprise Tunnel

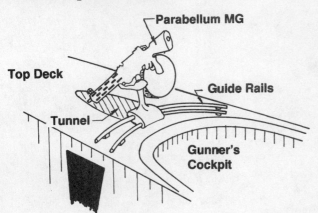

Parabellum MG

Top Deck

Guide Rails

Tunnel

Gunner's Cockpit

By shooting through a tunnel to the underside, the blind spot problem could be eliminated, preventing McCudden type attacks. *Source:* original drawing; data input, PRO file #AIR 1/1000/205/5/1255.

fewer hits when in the flexible arrangement, for shifting the greater mass precisely proved to be too demanding. Pull-down guns, after early success, faded in favor of twin fixed guns and great engine power. A practical means of shooting through a fuselage tunnel helped eliminate the classic two-seater blind spot.

Despite progress, the basic gunnery problem remained unresolved: few if any could shoot accurately at any appreciable distance. Even so-called medium range (250 yards) was much too far for accuracy. Actually, 20 yards was just right. Anything beyond reduced gunnery to a matter of probability, possibility, and uncertainty. Finding the sweet spot required more than skill—superior performance was a must.

How was top performance drawn from primitive aircraft?

6

Performance

THE FIGHTER PILOT'S WISH LIST WAS LONG but compelling. His machine required enough speed to overtake or escape from an enemy. To intercept, he needed a high rate of climb. To duck out of trouble, diving at a high speed was a must. To attain the best of firing positions, maneuverability exceeding that of his enemy was necessary. To be flown by beginners, a stable, forgiving machine was crucial.

Strategic considerations weighed in. With management determined to take the fight to the enemy, range mattered. So did the many small, secondary factors such as the amount of prop wash assailing two-seater gunners firing in defense as the machine headed home, low on fuel and bucking a headwind. Everything mattered.

Partial armor saved lives, but weighed as much as four small 20-pound bombs, useful to plague enemy infantry. To the endless list of desirable characteristics—accepted whole, compromised, or traded off—must be added the most important of all: simplicity in manufacture. The basic plan was to swamp the Germans with aircraft, if possible with excellent aircraft, and if not, then with mediocre aircraft, but whether good or so-so, in numbers impossible for the Germans to match. The combined British and French production output for 1917–18 was roughly three times that of the Germans, an enormous numerical advantage not to be overcome, even if the Allied machines proved slightly inferior. The plan had merit. Only hopeless incompetence of Allied aircrew or designs could lose the air war.

By 1917, design was on a sound basis and any single

desired characteristic could be created by a competent engineer. The difficulty came when all the good things were wanted in the same machine, for many desired qualities opposed others. For example, high speed called for a big engine, and these were heavy. The resulting fast aircraft tended to be heavy, with a good potential as a diver, but little hope of being a good climber, or of offering good maneuverability, for these qualities called for low weight. In other words, one couldn't have it all.

It was necessary to set design priorities, but these had much to do with personal fighting style. How can speed be rated against climb? Who is to say which is more important? The obvious solution was to turn the decision over to a well-regarded fighter pilot as judge. However, even Richthofen proved an uncertain guide, at one point (May 1917) opting for speed, "the important thing in aeroplanes is that they shall be speedy," only to immediately turn about and offer all-out support to the Fokker triplane concept, a slow but highly maneuverable machine.[1]

British experts also changed their priorities. In late 1916, RNAS fighter pilot and analyst Flt. Lt. C. R. Mackenzie believed "speed at a height is the greatest asset a machine can have." As for maneuverability, "given speed, it is not essential."[2] Within months, the relatively slow but highly maneuverable Camel arrived and forced the establishment to change course. At war's end, an RAF survey found "unanimous opinion" favored rate of climb as "paramount" with "rapidity of maneuver combined with a good view" as next in importance.[3] Bitter experience had forced a reluctant acceptance by British and German planners. Climb, maneuverability, and view were the combat pilot's highest priority needs. All else—even speed—was secondary.

Great War fighter design is the story of how this came about, a history of ever-changing hopes and priorities. The full story is beyond our reach. However, something can be said about the lessons learned during the Richthofen period.

Richthofen's life as a fighter pilot spanned two years, starting in the spring of 1916. He arrived in time to catch the end of pioneering air combat. His first victory was gained with an early Albatros against an FE2b British pusher fighter, a prewar concept prepared with shooting needs receiving top priority.

At heart, the pusher notion featured a full time observer/gunner at the very front of the machine, given a wide

Wartime Aircraft Production: German vs. Allied

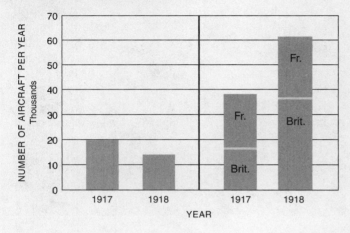

British, French, and German aircraft production for 1917–18. The Allies planned to swamp the German Air Service with numbers. *Source:* original plot from data PRO file #AIR 1/686/21/13/2252 and AIR 1/686/21/13/2248.

frontal firing zone with a superb view. No propeller blocked his gun, forcing the use of complex gadgetry to let bullets pass only when safe. The pilot served as chauffeur. A large engine at the fuselage rear pushed the package along on enormous biplane wings. Taking form as the Vickers FB5 and the Factory's FE2, the design persevered despite drawbacks, for here was a large, sturdy machine offering an effective gun platform. Slow and stable, the concept had merit.

However, the pusher propeller/engine arrangement, operating within air disturbed by passage of the fuselage, was 10 percent less efficient than a corresponding tractor. This was known before the war, when paying a 10 percent tax on power for good shooting seemed an acceptable price.[4] Use of rotary pusher engines upped the price to 15 percent and the beginning of concern. With the war came a heightened importance of fighter speed in pursuit and escape, encouraging an increase of the FE2b's stationary engine from 120 HP to 160 HP.

The competing Vickers FB5 was pushed by a rotary Monosoupape of 100 HP, an engine too small, too unreliable, and not readily uprated. The package wouldn't do— the machine was taken off frontline duties, leaving the FE2b as the primary British fighter.

Combat experience showed other difficulties. In a crash the rear engine mass was unstoppable, frequently crushing the pilot. Given a comparable tractor crash, the pilot's

The Disappointing Gun Bus

Combat proved the Vickers FB5's up-front gun to be a good idea, but the machine lacked the power to fight effectively. *Source:* original photo, RAFM, Hendon, London, United Kingdom.

chances were much better. As air combat slowly became a pilot's domain, the resulting bias against the FE2b grew ever stronger.

Even the shooting virtues of the FE2b came into question. In principle a two-gun fighter, the gunner had a free choice—front or rear—with the rear gun also serving for lateral shooting. However, using the rear gun was difficult, requiring the gunner to stand up without a harness, taking the full pressure of the air blast on his body, in order to fire over the top wing and propeller at a limited sector of sky. The process was too demanding and the profits too few. As a result, the machine was mostly used as a forward firing fighter, happily one without the maddening problems of gun synchronization delaying introduction of the Sopwith and BE12 fighters. In terms of performance, it was just good enough to stay in the air with its opponents (early 1916), and as a bonus, gunners were assured: "The rear gun mounting is also of use to keep off hostile machines in case [your] machine is so damaged as to render it necessary to fly straight home. If an enemy meets an attack and swerves at the last moment, a good opportunity is offered for a burst with the rear gun, but this must be given quickly and at close range, and no time must be lost in turning to attack afresh."[5]

Implication: if possible, stick with the front "attack" gun, for there's little chance of hitting anything from the rear gun mount. Although the rear gun seemed just right

FE2b Beardmore Aero

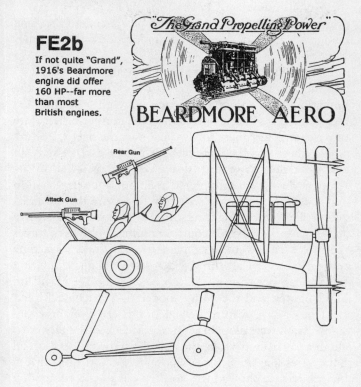

FE2b

If not quite "Grand", 1916's Beardmore engine did offer 160 HP--far more than most British engines.

"*The Grand Propelling Power*"

BEARDMORE AERO

Rear Gun

Attack Gun

Firing to the FE2b's rear required the gunner (front cockpit) to stand, turn about, and work against a powerful air blast, all while aiming upward over the top wing. *Source:* original sketch; advertisement, *The Aeroplane*, May 17, 1916, 771.

to beat off the favorite form of Fokker E-III attack—a dive on the enemy's rear—the probability of hitting the Fokker was small. Even if the gunner was able to cope physically, by struggling against the air blast from the knees up, only seconds were available before the E-III reached safety in the form of a lower, blocked-off zone. Once there, the FE2 propeller prevented direct rearward shooting. As officially admitted, "The worst defensive position is firing backwards over the rear plane against an attack from behind."[6]

Fortunately for the FE2, the tractor E-III and its follow-on next generation Albatros experienced shooting limitations as well, for they fired forward and only forward. Secondly, they lacked a gunner able to concentrate solely on shooting, instead placing the entire shooting burden on a very busy pilot. Finally, the synchronizing gear used to time bullets going through the propeller disc was capable of severe malfunctions, ending in a propeller shot to pieces. The E-III design in particular smacked of a too hasty development based on a race plane copied from the French—the Morane-Saulnier of 1912. Even the French prototype's prewar price, set slightly cheaper (5 percent) than the same company's Parasol, suggested understandable customer wariness.[7]

In contrast, the FE2b seemed a thoughtfully prepared and fully realized design. Plaguing the FE2 were not the limitations of a shotgun marriage between an outmoded race plane and a synchronized machine gun, but the failure of peacetime designers to visualize wartime needs. For example, there was the issue of built-in fore and aft stability and its terrible flaw: steep dives were impossible. Any attempt at diving was interpreted as an unwanted gust action and the enormous stabilizer cut in to restore the old horizontal flight path. Fighting off the stabilizer's corrective action with the elevator control required huge stick forces that not even the strongest pilot could maintain. Wartime testing led to at least three widely used designs exhibiting this strange behavior: the FE2b fighter, the De Havilland DH2 fighter, and the Army cooperation machine BE2c.[8]

The no-dive feature helped doom each of these designs. As all were slow machines, and lacked the power to climb away from trouble, the inability to dive closed off all hope of escape. A feeble, shallow dive could be realized, but experience showed this to be useless—the competing Albatros was much better at it.

Flawed or not, the FE2 aircraft was an important bulwark against the German challenge. At a time when little else was available, its performance, though deficient, managed to get by. For example, the 160 HP FE2b required just under 40 minutes to climb to 10,000 feet, where it developed 76 MPH.[9] The Fokker E-III offered a speed of 79 MPH at the same altitude, and a climb rate about twice that of the FE2b at lower, more common fighting altitudes.[10]

Gen. Hugo Trenchard, directing the RFC fighting in France, reacted to the disturbing performance deficit of his fighters by trying to avoid one-on-one confrontations. With his own priorities stressing army cooperation needs (range, reconnaissance, bombing), he saw air fighting as a secondary business, at most. The safe return of his machines was important, but he deemed convoys and formations the best way to assure survival, if possible through a process of overawing enemies with a display of collective firepower, rather than actual combat.[11] As for the destruction of enemy aircraft, yes, that too was important, and would become possible when the Royal Aircraft Factory de-bugged its next generation fighter, the BE12, a design reflecting the latest word, for it had both a tractor engine and a synchronous Vickers gun.[12] Until these were available, the FE2b and DH2, a lighter, single-seater pusher were deemed able to carry the fighting load.[13] Trenchard marshaled his FE2 fighters into formations and convoys, pressed the new single-seater pusher DH2 into action, and accepted strong French Air Service help, applied within the French sector in the form of the Nieuport Bebe. All taken together, the E-III was beaten off.

The event demonstrated Trenchard at his best. Here was a try-anything pragmatist, mobilizing whatever came to hand and making do with the mediocre. He did not find the process easy and there were many moments of despair. In time, the eagerly awaited BE12 was found to have a defective synchronizer design, a gun mount aiming the weapon at the wing drift wires, a defective magneto design, and finally the same excessive stability preventing a steep dive seen in the FE2.[14] Factory design impresario O'Gorman, so solid as an analyst, had failed as a design leader. As designer Geoffrey de Havilland, who knew him well, concluded, "[Some men] may be extremely good at managing a drawing office, have a good knowledge of mathematics and aerodynamics, and yet produce an aircraft fit only for immediate burning."[15]

Here was an excellent summary of O'Gorman: he was best at attending to a complicated detail, worst at overall design.

Finally reaching combat, many were shot down by Richthofen. A disgusted Trenchard, looking beyond the BE12, wrote Brancker in February 1917: "The German machines are increasing every week and are infinitely superior to ours. . . . I am perfectly certain that every FE2, FE8, and De Havilland Scout we have will be practically wiped out directly fighting gets serious. This ought to be easily seen by the number of casualties we are having now in FE's when there is practically no work to do [owing to bad weather]."[16]

His cry from the heart tells us more than any number of claims or communiqués. The German Albatros fighter series had changed the game and the pusher class of British machines were no longer competitive. As for the BE12—its stunning list of defects ended all hopes of a serious role in the Western Front war. What now, for 1917?

Bebe Replica

Perhaps it was maneuverability that really mattered most, and following this thought, the Sopwith Pup arrived, a marvel of well-behaved maneuverability, though with only one gun, too lightly armed, and with only 80 HP, too lightly powered. It was good at evasion but not suited for aggressive control of the skies.[17] Pilots, including McCudden, were delighted with its responsiveness and ability to fly within a small circle.[18] But as an air superiority machine—no.

Then the Sopwith Triplane, and while a useful machine, filling the need in some ways, it lacked the necessary maneuverability, speed, and firepower.[19] Representing a major increase in power, its 130 HP Clerget powered the machine with enough left over to permit a handsome rate of climb. Pursuing Albatros fighters could be left behind at last, not by speeding away, but by out-climbing them. Converting the altitude gain into a subsequent diving attack made the Triplane a serious contender. However, flaws ruled it out. Its single gun was a severe limitation, when matched against the two-gun Albatros. The extra gun advantage was much greater than the obvious two to one, for in high altitude combat at least one gun was likely to jam. In fighting at altitude, having a spare gun outweighed many other design attributes.

Finally, the Sopwith Triplane was subject to the same "reluctant diver" mode of flight noted above.[20] A cure, in the form of a smaller horizontal tail, was prepared by Sopwith. Experiments with an extra Vickers gun were also

This BE12 made the cover of *Flugsport* as captured booty, exhibited in Berlin. Note the unusual side-mounted Vickers gun just short of the cockpit. The enormous four-bladed propeller had advantages. Losing one blade out of four was a survivable event; whereas losing one out of two was not. *Source: Flugsport,* March 1917, front cover.

under way when the entire concept was phased out, a victim partly of innate inferiority and of growing confidence in its younger sibling—the Camel.

The Camel fighter seemed much like the proverbial Camel animal—a horse designed by a committee—in this case consisting of owner Tom Sopwith, test pilot Harry Hawker, and chief designers Fred Sigrist and R. J. Ashfield, with the Navy as a powerful advisor.[21]

Readying a Pup

A replica Sopwith Pup, preparing to take the air at Biggleswade air show United Kingdom. Note open center panel used to improve visibility. *Source:* original photo.

Sopwith Triplane

Sopwith's Triplane, a delight to fly, was judged safe, stable, and a bit too slow. *Source:* original photo, Biggleswade air show, United Kingdom.

Important to Sopwith's survival was an ability to duck crushing failures of the BE12 type. Sopwith existed to fill a need, not to strike poses. Given some sponsor agitation or a severe technical problem, Sopwith moved quickly. Its designers were practical, try-anything types. Suggestions soon became chalked lines on the shop floor, to be turned into real machines within weeks. Flexibility combined with a low-tech approach succeeded at a time when turnaround costs were low.

The Camel owed much to the Pup and can be likened to a Pup's mean-spirited younger brother. Where the Pup had only 80 HP, the Camel took over the Triplane's 130 HP Clerget power plant, an extremely well made rotary. With more power came the ability to loft two guns, usually twin Vickers. To fit the guns close together under the "hump," it was necessary to create right- and left-handed Vickers feed arrangements. Those who preferred a top-mounted Lewis gun were accommodated by eliminating one of the Vickers and throwing in a pull-down system for reloading.

Knowing that the Pup was just stable enough and liked, while suspecting that the Triplane was too stable and so would be disliked as "somewhat leisurely in maneuver," the Camel was moved oppositely—made deliberately unstable—in the hope of producing all-out agility—and respect.[22] The value of instability seemed confirmed because the Camel proved both highly unstable and extremely maneuverable, a judgment accepted as true by every Camel pilot. Far less certain was the net profit derived from such an arrangement—should such a dangerous machine have been tolerated?

Management was unsure and opted for both pro and con views by putting a competing but highly sane first line machine on its roster—the SE5a. Very much a product of Royal Aircraft Factory philosophy—stability comes first—the SE5a was created by a Factory group headed by Henry Folland.[23] Power available is always an early design issue and Brancker, seeking good fighter aircraft for his pipeline to Trenchard in France, started matters off by promising to supply the superb French Hispano-Suiza. O'Gorman, busy elsewhere, let Folland handle the development and a fine machine emerged in 1917, able, after receiving the usual power upgrades, to see the war through and most successfully at that.

The Camel

The Camel's pilot sat high over the gun fairing hump. Sporting twin Vickers and great maneuverability, the Camel proved one of the best, though also one of the meanest. *Source:* photo from Military Air Photos, Lincs, United Kingdom.

The very survival of the Camel and SE5a through and beyond the Richthofen era implies considerable merit. How could two machines with so different a set of genes each succeed? Let's consider these British fighter aircraft in depth, starting with performance—were they competitive with most German fighters?

Dividing all critical performance aspects into three areas —climb, speed, and maneuverability—much can be judged by checking the numbers. Some aspects of maneuverabili-

SE5a

The SE5a's long nose housed a liquid cooled 200 HP engine—powerful but vulnerable. Together with a stable layout, pilots were given a fast, steady gun platform, though not a very maneuverable one. *Source:* photo from Military Air Photos, Lincs, United Kingdom.

Fighter Climb Comparison

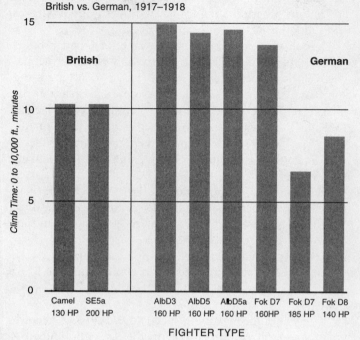

British vs. German, 1917–1918

The Camel and SE5a on test against their most likely opponents. *Sources:* original drawing from data, see chapter 6, note 25.

Y-axis: Climb Time: 0 to 10,000 ft., minutes (0, 5, 10, 15)

X-axis (FIGHTER TYPE):

British
- Camel — 130 HP
- SE5a — 200 HP

German
- AlbD3 — 160 HP
- AlbD5 — 160 HP
- AlbD5a — 160 HP
- Fok D7 — 160HP
- Fok D7 — 185 HP
- Fok D8 — 140 HP

ty do require something more—expert opinions of pilots—but these are on hand.

Let's start with climb, specifically, that maximum climb rate experienced over the entire altitude range from sea level to 10,000 feet, a matter of clocking the least time required for arrival. Good climb performance results from a nose-high, slow flight, all at maximum power while uncomfortably near stall. Pilot perceptions of what constitutes near stall varies, especially so when the machine has vicious spin characteristics, suggesting that stall be approached with great respect. The human element matters and we must accept as inevitable pilot-to-pilot variations in climb rate measurements. Although all the quoted results for British and German machines were gathered at the same experimental flight station (Martlesham Heath, United Kingdom), pilot-to-pilot, day-to-day variations must be expected.[24] Throw in British ignorance concerning details of German exotic fuel usage (Benzol plus alcohol). and British/German comparisons must not be pushed too far.

Still, Camel and SE5a climb performance was superior when compared to garden variety 1917–18 German fighters

—those powered by the 160 HP Mercedes. However, the later version of the Fokker D7 equipped with the 185 HP (D7F) was a better climber than its British opponents, as was the Fokker D8.

A look at the quantity of these superior German fighters is useful, for if too few, no matter how effective the machine, little influence could be felt in a conflict involving some thousands of machines. Both came on stream in the middle of 1918. Added to the roster were twenty-eight D7Fs in June, with production increasing to forty in August.[25] A few D8s were accepted in August, but were soon withdrawn for modification. Only a handful of D8s actually saw combat.[26]

With intensive combat winding down in October, these few superior machines couldn't have influenced the war. Much has been made of these new breed designs, and indeed they were excellent; however, they were too rarely met to play a significant role. As for the usual 1917–18 German fighter aircraft: in terms of climb, both the SE5a and Camel equaled or bettered their most likely opponents.

The values for maximum speed at 10,000 feet, recorded in standardized British testing for the entire Albatros series, ranged from 99 to 102 MPH, with 110 MPH measured for the 160 HP Fokker D7. The Camel reached 111 to 113 MPH and the SE5a had a top speed of 121 MPH. The SE5a and Camel were as fast or faster than their most probable German opponents.[27]

Was it a matter of engine size, of raw power? Checking engine size, note that the British engines were both larger (SE5a: 200 HP) and smaller (Camel: 130 HP) than the German (Albatros: 160 HP) engines. It follows that raw power alone doesn't explain British superiority.

Nor did those windage losses experienced by rotary engines clarify matters.[28] The superior climb of both the Camel and Fokker D8, despite rotary engines, testified to overriding factors. Of these, most important was drag, and specifically that drag developed when in extreme attitudes—near stall for climb, and near zero incidence for speed.

The answer then, to the source of good SE5a and Camel climb performance was one of high climb efficiency; that is, when at full power in a nose high, reduced speed attitude, the power consumed was low. Low drag was also evident when at small incidence, as proven by the superior

Camel Rotary Engine Windage Loss

Air drag produced by rotating engines led to a considerable power loss, in effect a tax on engine power, cutting both speed and climb. *Source:* original photo, RAFM, Hendon, London, United Kingdom.

**15.5% HP Loss
@ Max Speed**

**9.7% HP Loss
@ Max Climb**

speed performance figures. Summing up: flown either nose up (climb), or down (speed), the SE5a and Camel were unusually efficient, low drag machines, certainly more so than their usual opponents.

An important shooting bonus was offered to efficient climbers—a smaller turning radius, critical in holding the inside track in a turning contest. Circling in pursuit of an enemy favored the machine capable of shooting from the inside—the outside man couldn't align his sights on an inside target—and every pilot wanted a machine capable of holding the tightest possible circle short of losing altitude.

Many factors enter into tight circling. The ability to fly slowly counts greatly. Here the weight borne by every square foot of wing area—the wing loading—serves as a good index of slow flight ability. Lighter is slower and tighter. However, light machines lacking power and offering high drag tend to sink at a high rate when in a tight circle. As discovered by German engineers (1918), a better measure of practical, nonsinking, tight circling radius reflected max climb qualities—whichever machine offered lowest drag when at high incidence emerged as the winner.[29]

German researchers used the Siemen Schuckert Works D4 to examine practical circling issues.[30] Employing a 200 HP rotary and offering a superb climb, the pursuit circle was clearly to the machine's taste. Investigated was the effect of altitude upon the pursuit circle. Certainly engine

Climb Rate vs. Speed

Lt. A. Ball's preference for the Nieuport was reasonable. It offered a powerful gain in climb rate near stall—the key to turning in a small circle without sinking. Here was a formula for victory. *Source:* original plot of data PRO file #AVIA 6/1296.

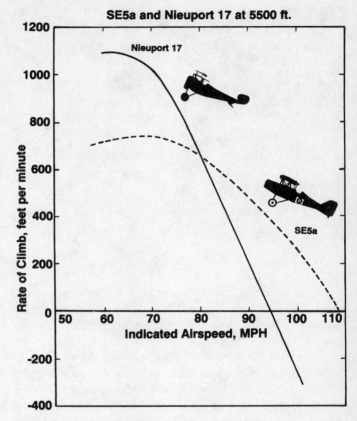

power output decreased with altitude. How did minimum turning radius respond? The answer: minimum radius increased with altitude; the machine demanded an ever-larger circle as it headed upward. At 10,000 feet, minimum radius expanded by roughly 60 percent, compared to its sea level value.

What about angle of attack?[31] Granted that the pilot must hold the wing at an optimum value in order to trace out the minimum diameter circle, how fussy was the demand? In practice, getting incidence just right meant hitting exactly the right speed, for velocity was the simplest indicator of nose-up or -down attitude. Did an error of a few degrees of angle of attack, or a few MPH really matter?

The answer was of the yes-and-no type—much depended on the altitude. At most fighting altitudes, say 0 to 10,000 feet, there was a fair tolerance for error. At 10,000

Tightest Turn Radius

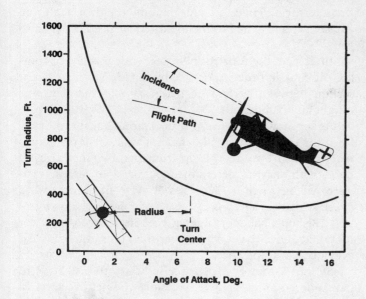

SSW D4 at 10,000 ft.

The tightest circle came from the 12 to 14 degree angle of attack range. Outside these values, the circle opened and the battle might well be lost. *Source:* original plot from data, chapter 6, note 29.

feet, the optimum angle of attack extended from about 11 to 14 degrees—far removed from the high speed range and yet not too close to stall—a zone that experienced pilots were able to locate with reasonable accuracy. However, as altitude increased still further, moving toward the ceiling, achieving a minimum radius made ever-greater demands for angular precision until the allowable angle of attack error became tiny—a matter of half a degree or so. No pilot could hope to meet this standard. To fight a circling battle at extreme altitude meant a fair chance of losing, despite high skill and a good machine. Squeezing out maximum performance demanded more flying precision than any man could offer; luck ruled, not skill.

Also studied was the matter of a fast turn versus a short turn. Perhaps a machine, by flying faster on a longer route, could beat a slower opponent moving on a smaller circle. The practical answer was yes, the smaller circle could at times be beaten, but only by a tiny amount, too small to matter in the real world. To win a circling contest, it was sufficient to fly the smaller pursuit circle, but even granted a superior machine, this was not easy. Lt. Oliver Stewart, fighting an Albatros with a Pup, reported: "I turned and turned and the Albatros turned with me, sometimes coming up to the Pup's tail so that I almost felt the gun fire in my back, but then falling behind again as I held height. It was a terrifying circus. . . . All the time the turn had to be adjusted and matched to the indicated airspeed. I began to gain."[32]

In despair, the Albatros pilot made the mistake of coming off bank in order to reverse his circle. A short straight section between circles was necessary and there he was caught and hammered.

As for Stewart's concern over indicated airspeed, it offered the single best clue to angle of attack. Pilots in combat were too busy to read instruments, but in a circling fight, with survival determined by angle of attack, men were willing to turn their eyes away from an enemy to check velocity as a necessary means of guiding their control stick. Bishop's Nieuport fighter, with its airspeed indicator mounted above the cowling, near the gun sight, was clear evidence of this practice.

Stewart's combat experience indicates the Albatros to have offered an acceptable, certainly competitive level of maneuverability. Oddly enough, the official British test of a captured specimen (version D5; tested October–November 1917) reported a less satisfactory state of affairs: "The machine is rather too slow to maneuver . . . the machine can be made to loop, spin, roll, etc. satisfactorily, but does so rather slowly . . . machine tiring to fly—heavy on stick."[33]

In short, the Albatros could do it all, but only in good time, without the urgency that combat demanded. McCudden's fighting experience taught him to be more respectful. He believed the Albatros to be every bit as maneuverable as his SE5a, and quoted personal encounters to back his position.[34] We accept McCudden's judgment as more accurate—SE5a maneuverability was likely equaled by the Albatros.

In contrast, Camel maneuverability was legendary: it was truly outstanding. At twisting and turning, the Albatros couldn't compete with the basic 130 HP Camel, much less the advanced version (150 HP Bentley). As given by Camel pilot Lt. Leonard H. Rochford: "I never met a German fighter which could out-climb me, though some of them were faster on the level and in a dive. None could out-maneuver the Camel."[35]

However, there were offsetting Camel deficiencies, and many German machines emerging late in the war were better all told, including the SSW D4, Fokker Triplane, Pfalz 12, and Fokker D7F. Concerning the latter, Ltn. Karl Degelow believed the D7F's "are also faster and more maneuverable than the Sopwith Camels."[36] To be faster was believable; to be more maneuverable was not. Yet, there was a certain truth in his claim. The "new brand" D7F,[37] offering a vastly improved climb rate of 1,400 feet/minute,[38] and highly maneuverable as well, was likely the war's best all-around fighter design. Although it caused great concern, the Fokker Works D7 production average (all versions) of roughly ninety machines per month (April 1918–November 1918) was slender indeed, and despite output bolstered with the aid of subcontractors, the totals remained small compared to the Camel output of roughly 5,400 machines.[39]

Another German design superior in certain respects—climb and maneuverability—was the Fokker Triplane, so strongly championed by Richthofen himself.[40] Especially gifted at flying a pursuit circle, the fighter produced this bitter comment from Maj. Edward "Mick" Mannock reflecting his SE5a experience: "Don't ever attempt to dogfight a Triplane on anything like equal terms as regards height, otherwise he will get on your tail and stay there until he shoots you down."[41]

While good advice, the Fokker Triplanes had weak points; for one, a limited top speed, and so could be beaten by refusing to fight on the Triplane's terms, much as World War II's Japanese Zero could be defeated by P-40 pilots refusing to fight a circling contest. Of course, any such combat constraint was worrisome. But as SE5a ace Lt. Bill Lambert commented, "They [D7Fs] were much better than the Triplane but we found that the SE5a could handle them."[42]

His many SE5a victories support Lambert's confident view, and we are left with the sense that an SE5a, flown and fought shrewdly, was roughly as good—though not superior—to its better opponents. As for the German conclusion concerning their Triplane experience: the three-wing concept was shelved shortly after Richthofen's death in April 1918, with fewer than 350 machines constructed.[43] So small a total—amounting to only 7 percent of Camel production—shows far greater German confidence in Fokker's competing D7 biplane.

Another advanced German fighter, the powerful SSW D4 noted in connection with circling studies, featured a

Notes on Scout Tactics

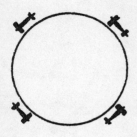

Maintaining a strong defensive formation, as shown, was another virtue of tight circling. *Source:* translation from German original by British Intelligence, PRO file #AIR 1/628/16/15/360.

radically novel engine. Difficulties with the tricky gearing of its rotary engine plus severe engine lubrication problems slowed development. Only a few examples saw combat.

In short, production of better-quality German machines never reached that critical mass required to sweep all before them. It was the Camel and SE5a that arrived in time and in sufficient quantity to determine 1918's outcome. To win, it wasn't necessary to have the best fighter plane. Victory went to the side flying good enough machines, serving in enormous quantities. The SE5a and Camel were those good enough machines.

Could the British have fared better? Although they possessed a winning formula, their victory came at a high cost. Had their machines been clearly superior as combat aircraft, the cost burden would have been lower. Were hordes of good enough machines really the best that the British aeronautical establishment could provide?

In 1917, though pleased with SE5a prospects, the Factory ran a study on possible improvements.[44] Noting the performance increase in moving from the prototype SE5, given 150 HP, to the 200 HP SE5a, an obvious question arose: suppose the engine power was raised further—what would happen to performance? Specifically, it proposed a 400 HP version of the SE5a mounted within a stretched airframe. Was there a profit in this notion or not? Should it be pushed? To lend reality to this imaginative design, a tough constraint was put into place: the resulting machine was to offer a maneuverability equal to the SE5a. The resulting design study offers a sense of contemporary thinking.

More power demanded more overall weight for the engine and structure, but the calculated weight increase wasn't that severe, and the 1917 designer anticipated a 1,200 feet/minute climb rate. Predicted speed went up as well, with an increase of 8 percent in prospect. All seemed fine.

Problems came with maneuverability requirements. Reasoning correctly that wing span had much to do with speed of banking (i.e., rolling), and that wing loading had much to do with the size of the smallest turning circle, the designer sought to retain maneuverability by keeping both the SE5a span and wing loading unchanged. To hold the line on wing loading, while accepting a major weight increase, a large increase in wing area was necessary. As a solution, the designer upped the chord of both biplane wings. This produced some uneasiness, for as he put it, the

Stretched SE5a

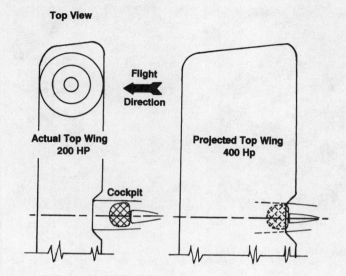

Top View

Flight Direction

Actual Top Wing 200 HP

Projected Top Wing 400 Hp

Cockpit

Feasibility study: why not an SE5a with 400 HP? The broad wing led to severe problems of drag and vision. *Source:* original drawing from data PRO file #AVIA 6/1169.

redesign "will probably change the wing characteristics to some extent."[45]

The aerodynamic effect of the change to a broad chord wing was understood only after the war. In brief, when in slow flight at the high angle of attack necessary for tight circling, broad, short span wings produced a ruinous increase in drag, as compared to narrow, long spans. When circling tightly, the stretched design's high drag acted to offset the gain in thrust produced by its larger engine. For circular combat, the broad chord stretched design was a sure failure.[46]

Not understood at the time, attention instead centered on a more obvious problem—vision. Unusually good in the SE5a, the planned change to a broad chord made matters impossible, cutting off the forward/upward view.

The visibility problem was considered important enough to warrant a separate study.[47] Suppose the upper wing's center section panel was removed—what then? Certainly vision would be much improved, but at what cost? In wind tunnel tests, the upper wing was chopped into two pieces, and each given neat, raked ends. As a result, there were four wing tips rather than the usual two. However, as would be learned after the war, when at a high angle of attack, huge drag losses occur at every wing tip. Doubling the number of wing tips wasn't a good idea. British test

SE5a Upward View

The good forward/up-ward vision of the SE5a depended on the wing chord. Expansion meant blockage. *Source*: origi-nal photo, RAFM, Hen-don, London, United Kingdom.

results for the open top wing pointed to a drag increase of one-third, when circling at the optimum pursuit curve incidence of 14 degrees.[48]

One-third more drag wasn't the idea at all. Common sense ruled: the wing wasn't to be split and given more tips.

Design studies are trial horses—cheap ways of testing strange notions. Implementation is problematic. The usual result is a bit more knowledge about a hard world. In this case we are left with a sense of how crippling was the period's aeronautical ignorance.

Although a tight circle does call for a light wing loading, more is involved—a whole body of knowledge called induced drag, unknown at the time. Chopping away the center portion of a wing was at best a poor idea, but given the tight circle requirement, it was a hopelessly bad idea. Today, designers know these things. In the spring of 1917, most aeronautics was uncertain. Enough was known to attain a single goal, for example speed, but the sophisticated understanding required to blend multiple goals, each bearing opposed requirements, for example speed and maneuverability, simply didn't exist. As a result, the design of each nation's fighters had as much to do with intuition and chance as with science.

Finally, there was always the hope of a fresh approach—a brainstorm leapfrogging all difficulties. In this case, rather than split the wing, why not keep it whole and simply cover the wing structure with transparent plastic to gain visibility? Such plastics were known and widely tried

Better Visibility SE5a

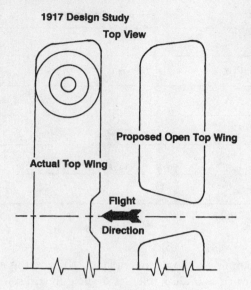

1917 Design Study

Top View

Proposed Open Top Wing

Actual Top Wing

Flight Direction

Experiments with an open center section top wing led to unacceptably high drag. *Source:* original drawing from data PRO file #AVIA 6/1208.

in the search for visibility. Advertisers cried their merits in the aero journals. Surely there must be some merit in the notion?

The SE5 design team mulled over the prospects of ever attaining that hoped-for 400 HP engine; they thought hard about drag, vision, unconventional wing covering materials; and gave up. It was too chancy, too big a leap, had too many uncertainties, and there was too little time. The SE5a would see the war through; as it was, it was good enough.

The Camel too would see the war through, though it earned the jibes of many a proud SE5a pilot. For example, there was Capt. Elliot W. Springs who sneered, "That's one thing about a Camel; you've got to shoot down all the Huns to get home yourself. There's not a chance to run for it."[49]

There was enough truth to sting—certainly the Camel was slower than the SE5a—yet each of the two machines was adequate, well able to compete against their usual opponents. Each not only satisfied official demands for "climb, rapidity of maneuver combined with a good view," but sold at midlevel prices, implying a bearable cost in man-hours.

Given the draft, with limited available labor, producing thousands of fighters was a difficult task. In this impatient atmosphere, any design offering production complications

How Much?

Reasonably low aircraft prices meant an acceptable number of labor hours per machine. This was the key to assembling a huge air fleet despite a tight labor supply. *Source:* original chart from data, Jones, *War in the Air,* appendix, vol. 7, 155–57.

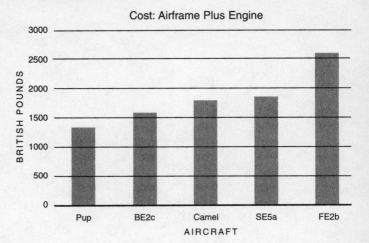

Cost: Airframe Plus Engine

—for example the Sopwith Triplane's six working ailerons —was viewed as undesirable. Its single gun and stately maneuvers were last straws. Wanted were good fighting qualities in no-nonsense, readily constructed aircraft. This was the package offered by both the SE5a and the Camel. Certainly, there were problems with maneuverability (SE5a) and stability (Camel), but wars are won not with the best but with the best available machine in quantity.

We accept the notion that climb and maneuverability were difficult to achieve, for these depend on many complex factors, some not understood at the time. Vision is different—it seems appealingly straightforward; yet as the next chapter will show, many problems arose in designing a "good view."

7

Vision

TO SEE THE OTHER FELLOW FIRST WAS every fighter pilot's goal. He could then evade safely or strike without warning. His obvious need gave birth to a pre-war panacea: a clear plastic covering promising invisibility, in the belief that you can't see that which is transparent. The dream was lost to sunlight glancing off the plastic, startling observers with blinding reflections drawing attention thousands of feet away.

Changing their approach, manufacturers pushed for inclusion of small see-through panels to aid vision, only to be caught out by the unsuitable nature of clear plastics. Too brittle for rib-stitching and subject to attack by fuel, the

Attempting the Invisible

Fokker's celluloid covered E-III seemed pleasingly ghostly and hard to spot—until it caught the sun. *Source:* photo from www. geocities.com/Times Square/Zone 4914/ images.

Could Celluloid Help?

"NONFLAMOID"
REGISTERED
NON-INFLAMMABLE CELLULOID
FOR
WIND SHIELDS, WING COVERINGS
OBSERVATION PANELS, & MAP COVERS

SPECIAL NOTICE.
We have on hand a considerable quantity of "Nonflamoid," in strips, 48in. × 7in., and can consequently give immediate delivery of Windscreens or Panels of dimensions not exceeding the above.

ALWAYS FIT "NONFLAMOID"

There will always be an ad-man, and Nonflamoid's pushed the use of treated celluloid; at best, successful for small surfaces. *Source:* Aeronautical Engineering Supplement to *The Aeroplane,* January 16, 1918, 328.

Although offering a splendid skyward view, the Bristol monoplane was blind to everything beneath. Chopping a window into the wing offered some relief. *Source:* original photo, RAFM, Hendon, London, United Kingdom.

use of clear celluloid or cellon presented many problems.

Inventors and dreamers jumped in. Soon there was a celluloid derivative claimed to be noninflammable, and an unbreakable safety glass, each pushing for the right to serve as wing covering.[1] Some limited success was achieved; for example, a transparent panel was used to cover the Sopwith Pup upper wing center section.

However, even this partial, compromise application proved iffy. Given bitter cold, the Pup see-through wing panel cover was prone to failure by "bursting in the air, with speed and climb so reduced that I could not catch up."[2] Despite ongoing problems, small transparent panels continued to be used throughout the war, for the most part signifying designer desperation, rather than user satisfaction.

Why the vision problem at all? Low air speed demanded a large wing area to generate sufficient lift. The typical Great War fighter was slow, and required a great deal of wing area. All that area forced a severe decrease of vision. Next, it was necessary to drape that area around the main

Bristol M1c

Measuring Blockage

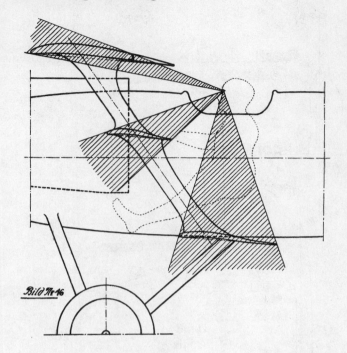

Bild № 46

Measured views were the standard means of evaluating a design's blind angles, as in this 1917 study of a triplane. The tiny middle wing chord added little blockage. *Source:* Aloys van Gries, "Dreidecker Gegen Zweidecker," *FlugM Tech. Berlin,* vol. 1 (Berlin, 1917), illustration 254.

weights—engine, pilot, and fuel. The resulting designs blocked off whole sectors of the sky, no matter how ingenious the designer might be. Even a clean monoplane arrangement, for example, that of the Bristol M1c had severe limitations. As the photo shows, its pilot was blind to any threat located near and below.

The standard tool in assessing this problem was measurement of the blind angle, sometimes taken from the top view to best describe flexible gun limitations, or pictured in a side view to make clear the pilot's problems. By simply adding all the blind angles for a design, one had as a total a measure useful for comparison purposes.

As an example, compare the Bristol M1c with another unusual layout, the De Havilland DH5. This machine, a biplane, employed reverse stagger to yield a superb forward/upward view, one with no blockage in its preferred orientation. The catch consisted of serious blockage elsewhere: straight down, and upward to the rear.

For those who preferred the DH5's unlimited front view, certainly novel for a tractor biplane, there was another problem—the matter of back stagger and its aerodynamic effects. In brief, wings in close proximity disturb one

The DH5 tried to improve vision by locating its upper wing behind the pilot, opening the up-ward/forward sector. Even so, the total blind angle was about 6 per-cent greater than that of the M1C. *Source:* original calculations and draw-ings.

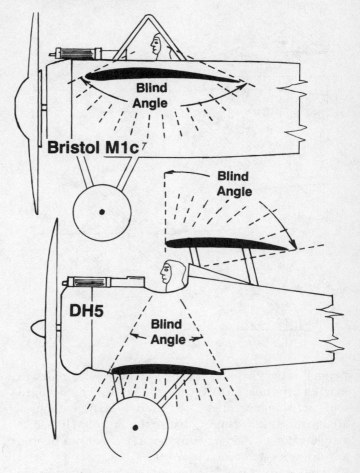

another.[3] No matter how arranged, some price must be paid for proximity, in terms of efficiency. Once the tax is paid (higher drag), conventional forward stagger has the virtue of acting in a slotlike fashion at high angles of attack, guiding air between the wing panels and so tending to delay stall, or perhaps granting better manners (less abrupt) to the stall event. Back staggered wings do the op-posite. The upper, rearward wing tends to be blocked by the highly turbulent flow streaming from the lower, near-stalled wing. Not only does back staggered performance fall off near stall, but the stick pressure feels wrong; the strange, labored redistribution of load on the wings is con-trary to the pilot's experience.

The result is a genuine performance loss at high inci-

Vision and Design

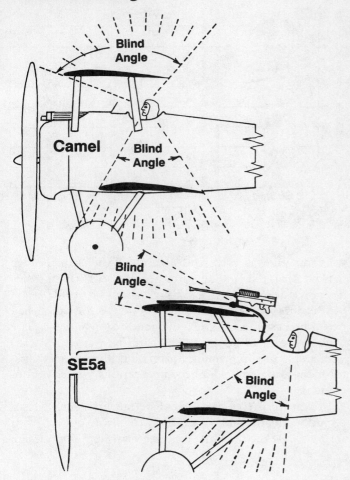

dence, as shown by a poor climb rate or ceiling, plus pilot uneasiness at the unconventional stick feel—a sense that elevator effectiveness diminishes progressively as stall approaches. To pilots trained on conventional biplanes, this apparent fading of stick power, just when most needed, is hair-raising. The DH5 was thoroughly disliked for both these traits, and never achieved a major role as a fighting aircraft.[4]

The Bristol monoplane offered its own set of problems. Although its performance was sprightly—123 MPH on the deck and 9.9 minutes to 10,000 feet (without a military load)—the test pilot's comment on vision was damning: "the view downward from the pilot's seat is bad and must be improved." In addition, there was great doubt that the

Fighter Blind Angle, Total

Comparing blind angle values, the SE5a emerges as the winner by nearly 60 degrees. *Source:* original calculations and plot.

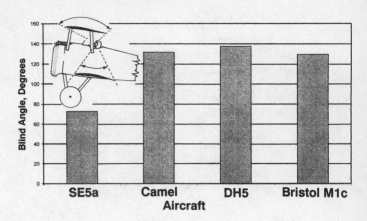

wing design was sufficiently sturdy: "when on a steep banked turn, the landing wires become so slack that they develop a deep bow . . . a sand test should be made."[5]

Reading between the lines: good performance had been purchased by trading away good vision and adequate wing strength. Although still early in the war (July 1916) with ample time remaining for revision, the efficient Bristol monoplane never did become a serious Western Front contender.

To modern eyes, the Bristol's clean lines spell air supremacy and the judgment of 1916 seems odd.[6] Yet, it wasn't so. At the time, the top four wants in fighter design

Superb Skyward SE5a Visibility

Another view of the SE5a pull-down Lewis gun, as seen from the upper wing. Imagine a pilot's head in position on the rest—his skyward vision would be excellent. *Source:* original photo, RAFM, Hendon, London, United Kingdom.

Lower Level SE5a Visual Clutter

Struts, cables, windscreen, and gun sights, positioned near the pilot, added up to a daunting blockage package. Source: original photo, RAFM, Hendon, London, United Kingdom.

were climb, maneuverability, vision, and speed. Of these, the Bristol's monoplane efficiency did offer a small plus in climb and speed. However, there was a steep price to be paid in the form of inferior maneuverability (slower roll) and poor vision. On balance, the package was unattractive. Something better was sought. Where vision was concerned, much better was wanted.

The search for something better in terms of vision was unending. Stubbornly returning to prewar dreams of invisibility, tests were conducted on a hapless BE12 fighter (February 1917), after recovering with the latest, improved celluloid material. Flight tests were conducted on a grim wintry day overlaid with ground mist, though the sky was clear. As the aircraft climbed through 4,000 feet, "the machine was only visible with great difficulty." All was well. But then, as it continued to climb, nearly vanishing at 7,000 feet, "its presence was revealed by a flash of reflected light."[7]

Nothing had changed. Slick plastics made for powerful reflectors. There would be no invisible fighter aircraft in the Great War.

Sharing the notion of visual fakery was the peek-a-boo gunner, playing dead to incite some aggressive attacker to close in. When near enough to permit accurate flexible gun shooting, the gunner would suddenly appear, just in time to hole his adversary. The following version, stressing chance, may carry some truth.

The Sopwith 1½ Strutter was a formidable two-seater

Peek-a-Boo Gunnery

Having retrieved his fumbled ammunition drum, a British gunner opens fire on an attacking two-seater lured into a close approach. *Source: The Aeroplane*, April 18, 1917, 958–59.

fighting machine, though the rear gunner was cursed with all the usual Lewis gun sighting and shooting difficulties. At a time within the period of Bloody April (1917), a German two-seater attacked a 1½ Strutter and was met with the usual ineffective Lewis gunner's return fire.

Changing drums in frantic haste while struggling against the wind stream, the frozen-fingered gunner committed the unforgivable blunder of dropping the replacement drum. As it hit the floorboards, the gunner dove for it, abandoning his gun. To the attacking pilot, the disappearing gunner was the expected response—the British gunner was dead—proven by the deserted gun, swinging about its pivot. Moving in for the kill, it was the German pilot's turn to be horrified "when up popped the gunner, having retrieved his dropped ammunition."[8] Now operating at a more desirable, closer range, the Lewis gunner prevailed.

Believable? Perhaps. It was at least true that mischance ruled at times, and even the apocryphal had its day.

However, the true point of the invisible covering and peek-a-boo gunner stories was the firm belief in vision or its negative opposite—invisibility—as winning tools. To some extent, magic thinking held rein. However, an air combat truth held center stage: it was crucially important to see the other fellow first. If one's own disappearance couldn't be arranged, then superior vision was the next

Sopwith Celebrates Christmas

SOPWITH

best thing. Unfortunately, bitter experience showed that really good fighting vision came with drawbacks; for example, the SE5a's superiority to the Camel in terms of vision was offset by inferior maneuverability.

As a cure, one might hope to better sluggish maneuverability with some last moment tweaking. Perhaps simple modification would do the trick, trading excess stability for badly needed maneuverability. Or was it all a matter of genes—pilot's genes? Nowhere was the uncertainty more evident than in combat itself, when gunning for the other fellow.

A vision of a different sort was offered by Sopwith's official 1916 Christmas card. Lack of pompous self-regard marked Sopwith; here was one company willing to try anything in a search for aerial supremacy. *Source: The Aeroplane*, January 3, 1917, 24.

8

Gunning for the Red Baron

WINNING AN AIR BATTLE REQUIRED MUCH in the way of gunnery, performance, skill, bravery, and luck. Less clear is the requisite proportion of each. How much was performance? How much was luck?

Consider two of Richthofen's battles, one early in his career and one that came last. In the earlier, we are able to follow the reasoning of the participants as they circle tightly, straining to settle gun sights on their opponents. In the last, leading to Richthofen's death, the clutter surrounding the event prevents clarity. Still, something can be said of the chances for success of three possible claimants for the role of victor.

In encounters between two enemy single-seater pilots sharing the same altitude, each automatically headed for his opponent's rear, hoping to find the enemy machine directly to his front. If a fighter pilot or machine was slow to respond, his speedier enemy could well earn an easy victory. However, if both opponents were equally alert and spry, neither found immediate success. Instead, the actual path traced out by the fighters became a spiral, narrowing down to a circle after many revolutions. Dogfighting was well named.

One classic battle, a fight between Richthofen and Maj. Lanoe Hawker (7 victories) in November 1916, illustrated the difficulties. Unlike so many battles between the skillful on one side and the inept on the other, each pilot was highly experienced and at the top of his form. The outcome reflected not only skill but also the influence of aircraft design, along with such unpredictable factors as wind direction and dumb luck.

Hawker's Oblique Firing Method

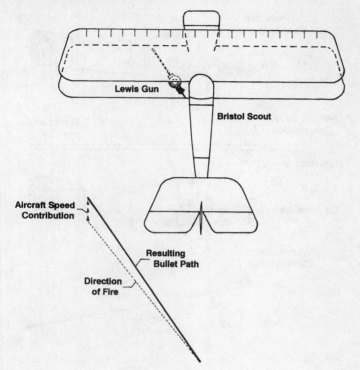

Hawker's Lewis gun used an angled muzzle to clear the propeller. Aircraft speed plus bullet velocity added up to a tricky resultant bullet path. *Source:* original drawing.

Hawker was one more military brat; his father a career officer in the Royal Navy. Attempting to follow, Lanoe was invalided out of Naval College with a breathing disorder related to a heart malfunction.[1] The Royal Engineers proved less fussy, and he graduated as a 2nd Lieutenant in 1911. Volunteering for flight training, he went to war as a low-time pilot, but one with real engineering aptitude, able to turn concepts into practical devices.

Addressing the problem of shooting in the air, he opted for a Lewis gun mounted to a single-seat tractor Bristol Scout, arranged to shoot obliquely so as to miss the propeller. The catch was a complicated bullet trajectory, one angled to his flight path and containing a sizable forward carry owing to aircraft speed. At a range of 200 yards, this forward shift in trajectory amounted to more than an aircraft length—too much to be ignored. Furthermore, the precise shift amount varied with Hawker's speed and the target range, making true accuracy most uncertain. While rear gunners also suffered these problems, they were able to make minute corrections to their aim by swiveling.

Accuracy and the DH2 Elevated Gun

Pushers (top) could fire directly to the front, simplifying bullet trajectory and easing gun sight usage. However, use of gun elevation (bottom) restored all the problems of angled speed components. *Source:* original drawing.

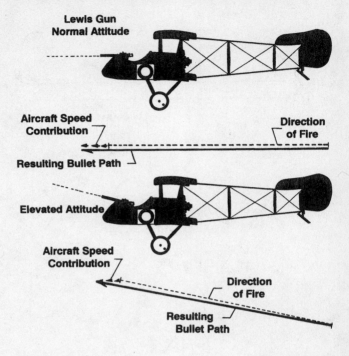

Hawker couldn't, for his mount was rigid. It was necessary that he redirect the aircraft to change the aiming point. Hitting anything with this rig wasn't easy.

Yet he was able to bring it off. The very first communiqué issued by the RFC (July 1915) described an encounter near Passchendaele (Ypres, Belgium) in which Hawker approached an unwary Albatros two-seater from down sun and opened fire at 100 yards. "The hostile machine burst into flames and turned upside down, the observer falling out."[2] Although not a true fight because "I had come upon him from behind unawares," Hawker got the job done and was awarded the Victoria Cross for his action, a first ever for air fighting.[3]

When experience proved his lateral firing rig a poor solution to the problem of accuracy, he welcomed the next generation of British fighters, a group featuring pusher aircraft, chosen for an unobstructed forward view and an up front firing point. Another virtue was the simple bullet trajectory achieved by its forward gun, when clamped to fire directly ahead. Lacking the dogleg, cross-eyed aspect of oblique fire, the resulting bullet velocity was merely the

The DH2

(top) A modern flying replica, realistic aside from the nonrotary engine. Sources: (top) Military Air Photo, United Kingdom.
(bottom) An authentic though gunless machine highlights the superb forward visibility. Rearward vision was poor. Source: www.geocities.com/jasta boelckeimages/dh2.

sum of muzzle velocity and aircraft speed. Bullet path was straight ahead, if flying straight ahead. Nothing could be simpler.

A born inventor and tinkerer, Hawker was unable to accept the DH2 (De Havilland 2) without attempting improvements. "Fug" or smelly hip length boots supplying high altitude warmth were likely his idea, as were revisions to the "double" Lewis drum, yielding a more field-worthy unit.[4] Other Hawker DH2 modifications included a means of unlocking the single Lewis on its mount to yield a flexible gun. However, flight tests soon showed that flying with one hand and swinging a gun with the other was too demanding a task. DH2 pilots settled for a partially adjustable gun, capable of elevation changes only. Official advice to pilots made much of this feature: "A good stratagem is to pretend not to notice a hostile aircraft diving on your tail. Fit a new drum, raise the mounting [i.e., increase gun elevation] and watching him over your tail, turn when he is about 400 yards off and give him the drum."[5]

Perhaps, but firing upward brought back all the uncertainties of oblique shooting, with its cross-eyed bullet trajectory. The likelihood of successfully bringing off the above stunt was low. As a substitute for either diving out of trouble or meeting it with a splendid zooming spiral, the official solution seems fanciful and forced.

The DH2 brought many disappointments. The machine was officially described as a nondiver, for reasons of excess stability. Those who persisted in diving the machine, by employing brute strength and then pulling up sharply, produced a wing collapse leading to death. Hawker's friend Capt. "Bim" Mitchell died in exactly this fashion with Hawker looking on. The inability to dive out of trouble was a serious disadvantage—every fighter pilot's favorite exit was closed to DH2 fliers.

The engine, a Monosoupape (i.e., single valve) rotary, was tricky and unreliable. The engine's blip switch controlled power crudely, offering either full power or nothing. While an aid to maneuvering, the lack of shading prevented smoothness. Low-time pilots, moving from full torque to zero and back again too quickly, sometimes became confused and spun in.

Yet there were virtues. The machine was light and agile. As a gun platform, it was good, offering a drum-changing routine much more practical than that of its contemporary, the remote gunned Nieuport 11. Hawker, by then a high-time pilot, wasn't threatened by DH2 oddities, and came to like it. He believed the machine could be put through almost any maneuver if one "flew the machine carefully round instead of pulling it back violently."[6] In other words, patience and delicacy paid. Perhaps, but patience and delicacy seemed a poor fit to the urgent demands of combat. That his fellow RFC fliers had little enthusiasm for the DH2 was not surprising.

RFC dislike of the DH2 increased when performance was considered—specifically the relative performance of the DH2 compared to the Albatros D2, a most likely opponent in 1916. Comparative flight test data made grim reading for the RFC.

Basic performance consists of two parts: speed and climb. A machine inferior in one respect can be doctored somewhat with a new propeller of different pitch, produc-

Albatross D2

ing a tradeoff between desired abilities. However, nothing can be done for a fighter plane inferior in both speed and climb aspects—such a machine is inferior and beyond hope.

Lacking speed, it can neither flee when attacked nor can it overtake, if in pursuit. Lacking climb, it can't intercept an enemy at a higher altitude. Climb rate is also a measure of another good thing: spare power, left over from the basic energy cost of flying. With spare power on hand, other combat virtues are available, such as acceleration.

Early Albatros fighters had a nicely streamlined entry and vertical interplane struts. (bottom) The slightly flattened fuselage sides of this D2 would be rounded in the next and most famous Albatros model: the D3. Source: both from Mil. Air. Photo, United Kingdom.

Even the ability to circle tightly depends on the availabilty of enough spare power, required to offset those extra large drag values encountered as the circle tightens. In short, performance is crucial to a fighter plane. Maneuverability alone won't do.

The climb performance of the DH2 was adequate at sea level, offering about 800 feet per minute, a respectable figure for its time. However, even at 5,000 feet, climb rate was reduced by nearly half. Still higher altitudes yielded an ever-greater fall off. At 10,000 feet, true combat became impossible, for the necessary spare power no longer existed.

In contrast, though the Albatros D2 started its climb-out from sea level at an inferior 700 feet per minute, it was able to maintain values close to this rate at 5,000 feet. Even the subsequent falloff, on the way to high altitude, continued to be modest. At 9,000 feet, with the Albatros D2 offering twice the climb rate of the DH2, it would have been most unwise for any DH2 pilot to accept combat from an Albatros D2. Only extraordinary luck or skill could offset the debit of performance.

Moving DH2 combat downward, all the way to the deck, might seem a solution, for the machine's climb was slightly superior to the Albatros D2 near the ground.[7] Granted this advantage, upon turning to speed DH2 pilots found a new hurdle. Like most aircraft, the DH2 experienced maximum speed at ground level, in this case an officially timed 93 MPH.[8] However, a captured D2 yielded 100 MPH under RFC test—a large difference—and one in favor of the Albatros.[9]

To sum up: combat success depended greatly on performance. DH2 pilots, at altitudes exceeding 2,000 feet, suffered both an inferior climb and a much lower speed as compared to the Albatros D2. It followed that at higher altitudes, unless his skill was much superior, a DH2 pilot had little chance. However, at ground level, though deficient in speed, the advantage in DH2 climb rate did offer some prospects for winning.

Aware of their machine handicaps and the odds, shrewd DH2 pilots headed for the deck when engaged in combat. However, their descent was a cautious one, subject to a limited diving speed, for fear of causing wing failure. Wise Albatros D2 pilots sought to fight their battles at a higher altitude, where their performance was best in every respect.

Basic procedure in a circular fight consisted of first converging on a small flight path diameter and then pushing

Climb Performance: DH2 vs. Albatros D2

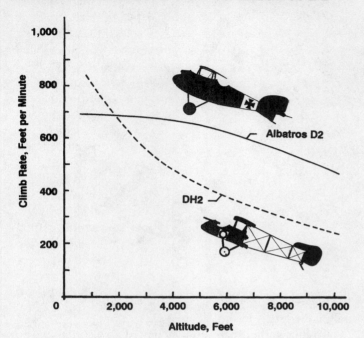

Inferior climb perform-
ance at high altitude
was especially trouble-
some for DH2 pilots.
Source: original plot from
data, chapter 8, note 7.

for either a spiral or a circular tactical solution.[10] Consider
an example of spiral tactics, as shown on the next page. Assume the Albatros D2 to be circling tightly, struggling to
line up its sights on a DH2 (position A). However, the
DH2 is circling just a bit too tightly to enter the Albatros
sights. Shooting produces misses toward the outside of the
circle. The Albatros may be tempted to rudder toward the
center of the circle, believing his sights will move toward
his elusive enemy. They will—but only horizontally. As for
the vertical, his drag will increase greatly because of the
newly yawed flow striking his fuselage. The result will be an
instantaneous drop in elevation. In a relative sense, the
DH2 will move upward, out of the Albatros sights. For
this reason, kicking in yaw as a last moment correction
usually didn't work.

What might succeed is shown starting at position B
('Spiral Tactics,' p. 148) when the DH2 takes the offensive
by moving (positions B and C) toward the center of the
circle while simultaneously cutting speed, chancing stall
and spin. The more heavily wing loaded Albatros D2 can't
follow, and in a relative sense finds that its original circle

Spiral Tactics

To win this spiraling fight, the DH2 moves inward at B and slows down. His opponent becomes a good target at position C. *Source:* original drawing.

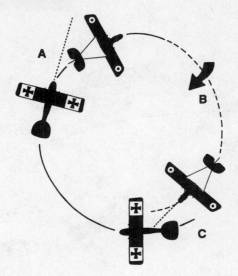

has become the outer track. In time (position C) the DH2 will find a target in the Albatros D2.

Circular rather than spiral tactics could also be used to set up a good firing position. One advantage going to the machine capable of tight circling is the right to exercise that ability in a secondary fashion by flying along a still larger circle at increased speed. High speed in a circling fight was hard to come by, for tight circles required slow speed. Only those with unusually good tight circling characteristics could afford to trade off some of that ability in order to fly a larger circle quickly. The DH2 was one of the few fighters able to do so.

Replaying the previous fight, consider a different form of counterattack by the DH2. This time, continuing to move along its basic circle, it simply speeds up. The Albatros D2 can't, for it's already at its smallest circle. To speed up requires it to move radially outward, yielding a spiral tactic defeat, identical to the preceding encounter. Yet, not to speed up means that given time the DH2 will ultimately catch up and assume a winning firing attitude ('Circular Tactics', p. 149, position C).

In short, given a circling fight, any machine finding it necessary to fly along a large turning radius was doomed. With so much depending on this one characteristic, designers gave it much thought.[11] Wanted was a lightweight machine equipped with a large wing area. Unfortunately such a design could not satisfy the opposing requirements

Circular Tactics

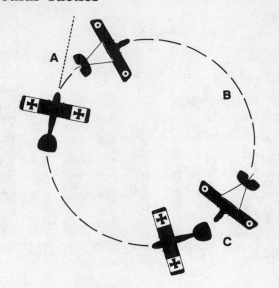

As before, the Albatros D2 is unable to line up on its target. The DH2, able to fly on a smaller circle, trades this advantage for more speed over a larger circle, ultimately arriving at good firing position C. *Source:* original drawing.

of speed, where a heavy (i.e., powerful) engine and a small wing area (i.e., low drag) were necessary. The sullen gods of compromise usually pointed to a machine offering neither speed nor a tight circle. Life for fighter pilots, as for all of us, was one of make do.

There was worse to come. Flying along one's theoretical circle is roughly equivalent to reaching one's theoretical age limit of 120 years or so. Getting there isn't easy. Few make it. In the case of circling, one major problem is that of centrifugal force.

Circling itself gives rise to an outwardly radial force, called centrifugal. Unless opposed, the result is a skidding action. Balance requires that one's wings be banked accordingly, canceling out centrifugal force with an opposing inward component. Banked roads accomplish the same thing for speeding cars, and as with cars, an increase in centrifugal force calls for more bank. Two new problems arise. First, the tipped wing must develop more lift, enough to balance out the new demands created by centrifugal force. As goes bank, so goes the demand for more lift until, at typical World War I combat bank angles, 30 percent or more of extra lift was required. The generation of extra lift was made especially difficult by the low speeds required to seek out the smallest possible circular path.[12]

Extreme wing loads and low flying speeds led to another practical problem—a reduction of ceiling. Lift generation depends on the local density of air. Under extreme

Theoretical Minimum Turning Radius

Turning radius mattered and the advantage of the DH2 over the Albatros D2 was significant. Note deterioration of later Albatros models—most disturbing to Richthofen. *Source:* original plot from computations in note 11.

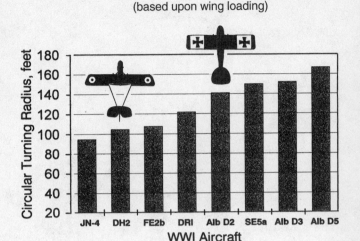

(based upon wing loading)

demand, upper altitude air is too thin to supply the necessary lift, and a steeply banked aircraft descends whether the pilot likes it or not. In effect, banking causes a cut in ceiling. The relationship becomes profound at 30 degrees—roughly 5,000 feet is lost; and moving toward 60 degrees, one sees that circular flight without descent was flatly impossible, given World War I aircraft performance limitations.[13] This particular relationship explains the mystery of why circular combat always moved downhill: steeply banked machines, unable to develop enough lift, descended despite all-out urging by their pilots.

Why did pilots care about lost height? On the one hand, the lower machine, flying with fixed guns at the edge of stall, couldn't risk nosing upward—preventing it from shooting at the upper machine. On the other hand, the machine on top had a fair chance at a shot, by simply nosing down and paying a price in altitude. In time the uppermost machine might hope to reach a point where it became profitable to abandon the circle and plunge into a dive, using the resulting gain in speed to position itself for a full deflection shot at close range. An alternate choice for spending one's altitude bonus—an even more attractive possibility—was a new circular path position immediately behind an opponent. So important was this possibility that pilots attempted to rate aircraft accordingly—in terms of ability to circle tightly, without appreciable descent.

Another major factor pushing for descent was drag. At

Why Circling Increases Wing Load

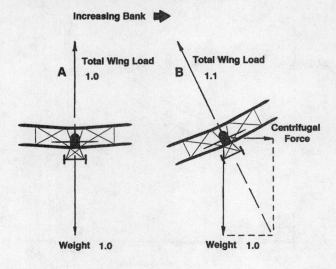

Bank, necessary to counter centrifugal force, creates a need for more lift to restore balance; the greater the bank, the more the lift is necessary. For the modest bank shown, a 10 percent greater lift is required. *Source:* original plot (See note 12).

Total Wing Load vs. Angle of Bank

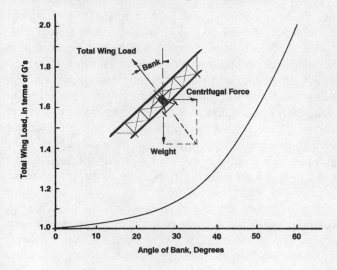

Wing load dependence upon angle of bank, expressed here in G's, can become disturbingly large, amounting to roughly 2 G's at about 60 degrees of bank. *Source:* original plot (See note 12).

the high incidence necessary for maximum lift production, wing drag became enormous. Great thrust was necessary to overcome the developed drag, and machines unable to develop the required thrust had no choice but to move downwards, feeding altitude into the kitty as a kind of tax on the poor. It paid to have plenty of thrust on board.

So important was thrust in preventing forced descent that it must be added to the other major controlling factors.

Ceiling Cut Owing to Circling Flight

Another disadvantage of steep banking is a lowered ceiling, the result of banked flight's demand for more lift; a demand satisfied only by descending into the thicker air of low altitude. *Source:* original plot (See note 13).

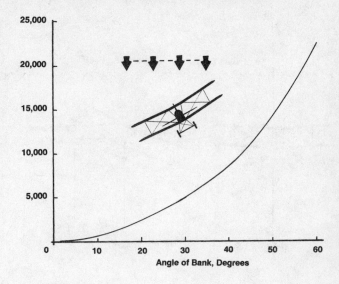

Our final list of sensitive inputs includes: wing loading, thrust, bank, and altitude. With four different factors controlling the result, it was unwise to take any one factor as the "key" to circling ability. An extremely lightly loaded wing, with a promisingly low theoretical minimum turning radius, yet lacking in sufficient thrust to pay for its small circle, could prove disappointing—either sinking at a fast rate or, if determined to minimize sinking, forced to surrender radius by moving radially outward. Given non-optimum flying conditions or a low thrust output, such a machine had little chance of reaching its projected minimum circling radius.

For a sense of the painful choices facing pilots trying to win a circling battle, see the plot, on the next page. Given are test results taken from Jenny flight data immediately after the war. The Jenny, though no fighter, was close enough to a true fighter plane to serve as a stand-in, and its near zero cost (war surplus) encouraged some interesting test work never performed with real World War I fighters.

Starting at a circular flight radius of—let's say 900 feet—our pilot finds banked flight at about 25 degrees and 80 MPH satisfactory (intersection, upper curve). The speed is safely high, the bank is satisfyingly low, and all is well. However, let's assume that his opponent can do better. To improve turning radius, our pilot has two basic moves. For one, he can (choice A) reduce speed while

Circling Radius: Bank vs. Speed

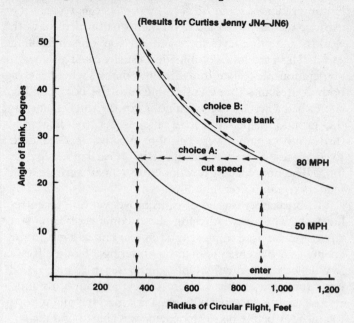

This Jenny stands in for a World War I fighter, offering its pilot a wide choice between speed, bank, and circling radius. *Source:* original plot from calculations, chapter 8, note 12.

holding bank. If pushed far enough (intersection, lower curve) he will reach roughly a 350-foot radius at 50 MPH. The improvement in radius is great. However, he is now perilously close to stall. Just a bit of misjudgment here and he will stall/spin out.

Had he made the other choice (B) and maintained his speed while increasing bank, the same radius would be attained at about 50 degrees of bank. While the higher (B) speed meant less danger of stall and more responsive controls, his new flight attitude taken together with the Jenny's slender available thrust assured a high rate of descent. Throw in the high G loading experienced at large bank, acting to inhibit gun jam correction/reloading, and we see that plan B, as well as A, produced highly negative side effects.

Of course, our pilot can choose compromise solutions—those many possibilities filling the large gap between A and B. However, each such solution will create compromise side effects as well. There is no way of wriggling out. At best, our pilot has only a choice between unhappy alternatives.

Although our pilot is already uncomfortable at his new radius of 350 feet, let us suppose that his enemy can circle more tightly. What then? Remembering that his theoretical limiting radius is about 95 feet, he presses on. To gain the extreme radius, he must take on the worst burdens of both worlds, accepting extreme bank on top of semistalling speed. This particular combination usually came about as a desperation move late in a circling contest, when one or both contestants threw everything into the pot. Coming late, it had a certain logic behind it, for the thicker air near the ground helped generate lift. As for the necessary thrust, most engines were far more effective near sea level. Even so, few aircraft could maintain a near knife-edge for long. The approaching ground was a final warning that matters couldn't continue.

To breakaway was an obvious move, yet one taken reluctantly. The awkward thing about coming off a pursuit circle was the need to present one's rear end as a gift to the enemy—an extremely dangerous offering of oneself as a low-deflection target.[14] Only the faster machine could hope for a reasonably safe breakaway. Although instantaneously exposed to enemy firing, a fast machine might hope to pull away before his slower enemy was able to find the target. If much faster, a tangent exit ('Breakaway Choices', p. 155, A) was quickest at promoting distance. By employing a somewhat slower curved path (B), pursuers were forced to employ deflection, and even a slight deflection correction led to many misses. For fast divers (C) a diving exit offered a neat and complete farewell. As for the necessary speed advantage permitting escape, a large difference in velocity alone wasn't enough. Acceleration mattered more, for it was the first few seconds of breakaway that counted most, and within the initial few seconds, rate of change of speed determined success or failure.

Acceleration had everything to do with driving force. When on the level, all depended on excess thrust—the same quality displayed in climb rate. In a dive, a high gross weight also proved useful in promoting speed. Of course, sturdy wings were a necessity, and here the Albatros D2, likely the best diver of the series, far outshone the DH2.

The DH2—a nondiver, slow at all altitudes, and a poor climber at higher altitudes—made for a poor fighting machine. Compared to the Albatros D2, its performance numbers were mediocre, if not hopeless. Hawker knew this; perhaps not in crisp numerical form, but as a series of generally negative DH2 traits. Yet as an officer he was part of management and could not take a position condemning

Breakaway Choices

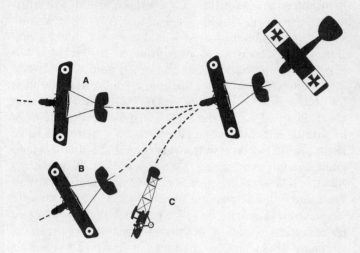

After abandoning the pursuit circle, one could (A) move along a tangent, (B) follow a curved path, (C) half-roll and dive. For the DH2, choice C was most unwise. *Source:* original plot (See note 17).

his own machine. Instead, one month before his climactic duel with Richthofen, he offered these views on the DH2:

> The French refuse pushers on the ground that if turned into tractors, their performance would be increased by 10%, but the good visibility and fighting qualities are more important for this particular work [DH2 speed deficiency relative to the Albatros D2 was about 10%]. . . . At present the enemy possesses the advantage in this respect [speed] and they are confident of their ability to run away [breakaway] from any one of our machines when they have had enough fighting. If they were chased right home once or twice, and worked under constant threat of our offensive patrols getting behind them, it is probable that their morale would rapidly collapse.[15]

He didn't explain how the slower DH2 was to chase its opponents home. As for morale collapse by German fighter pilots, his tactical plan to achieve this desired end was unconvincing at best. Hawker likely knew this, for he was no fool. Yet management needs—in this case a certain "rah-rah" or bravado quality he sensed as wanted—produced strange statements, even from Hawker, a highly rational man.

The Hawker/Red Baron battle started at about 8,000 feet on a typical cold and windy fall day (November 23, 1916).[16] With the prevailing wind blowing from the west, toward German-held territory, the weather favored Richthofen. Should he lose all power, he would land within his own lines. Not so for Hawker. Any lengthy time spent circling about in wind would carry the dueling machines miles downstream, away from the British lines. For Hawker, getting back would take much time and fuel.

Offering himself as bait, Richthofen dithered and waited for one or more of three visible DH2 machines to take up his challenge. Each of the DH2's had a considerable edge in altitude—Richthofen appeared to be a perfect bounce victim. A modest dive, well within the DH2's ability, would grant enough extra speed to keep pace with Richthofen's Albatros D2. For the speeding DH2 to assume the "50 yards and behind" position would then be easy. Although suspiciously generous, the offer of speed along with a free no-deflection shooting position proved most attractive. Certainly RFC attack instructions for the DH2 were clear: "When dealing with a slow scout like the DH2, it is necessary to get above the hostile machine and thus gain your speed by diving on him."[17]

Hawker stared downward at a seemingly perfect textbook opportunity. Of course, it could also be a trap. If so, he might detect trickery through sudden liveliness on the part of the bait, bursting into action just after his DH2 was committed. The bait's best countermove was a turn to face his descending enemy, combined with a rush toward the enemy's rear—the start of a classic pursuit circle. Hawker pondered—and dove.

It was a trap. Richthofen started his countermove circle, though just a bit late. Hawker was able to get off five shots —a standard test burst—from his single gun, but sensed that he was wasting his ammunition, with all the DH2 bullets going wide to the outside. Diagnosis: Richthofen was out-turning him. Hawker stopped shooting to concentrate on the critical business of circling.

At 8,000 feet the DH2 couldn't circle tightly—it lacked the necessary engine power. Although much more powerful, the Albatros D2 was handicapped with a higher wing loading. The two drawbacks were equally potent. Each pilot settled on roughly the same circular diameter and circled steadily, surrendering altitude at about the same rate. Neither was able to command a decent firing position. With breakaway always a dangerous move, clinging to a draw seemed a better bet. Especially so, when each reasoned that the draw would end in his own favor at some lower altitude.

Richthofen was so certain that thicker air would make him a winner that he questioned Hawker's judgment in refusing breakaway at 6,000 feet: "my opponent ought to have discovered that it was time for him to take his leave."[18] Acting against Hawker's departure was the gain in DH2 power anticipated near the deck, yielding an improved ability to tighten pursuit circle diameter, without undue sinking.

They continued to turn and sink for thousands of feet of altitude, always opposite, on the same basic circle. Ultimately, with their remaining altitude amounting to only hundreds of feet, sinking became unacceptable. The circular diameter at this point was judged to be 250 to 300 feet by Richthofen.[19] These numbers, roughly equal to the theoretical minimum (see minimum turning radius chart), implied an all-out effort—everything had been thrown into the balance.

Yet the draw persisted. Hawker's optimism was mistaken, as was Richthofen's. Neither could gain a decent firing position. Facing an approaching forced landing well behind German lines, Hawker was pressed into a breakaway attempt. Flying the slower machine, he tried for a zigzag path requiring a high deflection allowance from Richthofen's bullets. It didn't work. Hawker was shot dead within 150 feet of the front lines.

From Hawker's point of view, something had gone terribly wrong. Able to match turning circles at altitude, the expectation that he would do even better near the ground was a reasonable one. The known climb rate characteristics of both machines (see climb performance chart) backs this outcome. Yet his expected gain in turning circle radius didn't materialize. Most likely, the anticipated surge of power near the ground never happened, and with this failure, his battle was lost.

Hawker's brother, and biographer, pointed to an engine malfunction claimed as known to Lanoe Hawker just before the battle occurred.[20] Perhaps, but this hardly accounted for the DH2's solid turning performance at those higher altitudes encountered at the battle's start. Nor does it explain why Lanoe Hawker chose to give battle at all, if aware of a defective engine.

A more probable solution is that the 35-minute fight, all at peak revolutions, came as too much of a burden for Hawker's Monosoupape rotary engine. Loss of revs was a well known aspect of rotary life, developing over time as carbonized castor oil droplets coated valve seats, preventing

Hawker Engine Problems

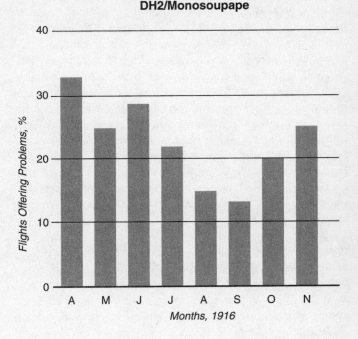

DH2/Monosoupape

valve closure, or stuck to cylinder walls, preventing piston rings from sealing. The net effect was to lose compression—and power—though the engine still ran. Hawker's loss was consistent with such a happening.

Had his engine held up, there is reason to believe that Hawker's circle would have narrowed to a winning extent at about the 1,000-foot level (see climb performance plot). Instead, once into the duel, his fading engine deprived Hawker of the thrust necessary to either out-circle Richthofen or to breakaway cleanly.[21]

In short, Hawker was doomed not by lack of skill or even by his generally inferior aircraft but by a lemon rotary engine. In the end, forced to rely on luck and the difficulties of deflection shooting for escape, he lost his bet.

Much as we all would do, Richthofen used his triumph over Hawker to confirm his own fixed views. Hawker was known to Richthofen as the English Immelmann, famous for novel tactics and aerobatics.[22] As it happened, Richthofen thought little of aerobatics and trick flying. The demise of Hawker served as neat self-justification. After all, what good had these skills done Hawker?

Chapter 8

To Richthofen, what mattered was possession of the better machine, one allowing straightforward tactics. There was a good deal to be said for Richthofen's approach. Unfortunately, it offered no place for the dull reality of carbonized castor oil droplets. In the end, few of us are undone by the grand strategies or superior skills of our enemies. It's the carbonized castor oil droplets that get us.

Exactly what finally brought Richthofen down remains uncertain despite the efforts of many historians. At least three full books and many articles have dealt entirely with this subject, and yet all end in uncertainty.[23] As with pilots Guynemer, Mannock, and many others, we know just enough to be skeptical of any solution. We turn away from the advocates, each pressing some conjecture upon us, backed with the usual pale evidence. We do not believe, for good reason.

What is a prudent observer to make of it all? Putting aside the bizarre, we are down to three possibilities. In a swirling dogfight extending to ground level, he was downed by either: (1) Camel pilot Lt. Arthur Roy Brown (10 victories), or (2) one of a group of Australian antiaircraft machine gunners, or (3) an unknown rifleman.[24]

Each possibility has drawn knowledgeable backers. The Brown solution was pushed by Billy Bishop; the Australian machine gunners by Lt. Elliot Springs; and the rifleman by Capt. Ira Jones.[25] However, nothing truly satisfies in this confused area. Key pieces are missing and no amount of advocacy can substitute for missing logic.

The over-supply of claims and views led Bristol Fighter ace Maj. Keith Park, later commander of No.11 group in the Battle of Britain, to comment: "I was the only Allied soldier on the Somme front who neither killed Richthofen nor saw him killed."[26]

Park's sardonic comment is valuable—too much nonsense has been offered us in the guise of eyewitness reports. Suspect views included those of witness Lt. W. R. May, the Camel pilot serving as Richthofen's immediate target, who pointed to his own Flight Leader Brown as victor. However, this claim was rejected by a number of ground observers who saw matters quite differently. Instead, they opted for one of several ground-based machine gunners as the true victor. As for the rifleman possibility, war experience has shown that bored, well-armed men were only too likely to fire at any low-flying aircraft.

We don't know what brought Richthofen down and

are unlikely to ever know. Instead, we are reduced to the uncertain world of possibility and probability. That said, what part did gunnery play in determining the odds?

One of the curious things about Richthofen's end is that only one bullet struck his body. For that matter, no other bullet can be proven to have struck his aircraft. Admittedly, such a determination is uncertain, owing to souvenir hunters who cut up and pocketed the Triplane's cloth covering within days of Richthofen's final landing.[27] Still, the engine survived. Although of a large volume well suited for catching bullets, and located within 5 or 6 feet of Richthofen, it shows no sign of a bullet strike.[28] It would seem likely that only one bullet reached the target's vital area.

Something about machine guns makes this possibility difficult to accept. Intuitively, we anticipate a spray of bullets as striking the target area—not just one. Conversely, the existence of only one bullet offers perfect support for the rifleman possibility; that is, only one bullet arrived because only one was fired. If indeed there was but a single bullet, are machine guns ruled out as the source?

Billy Bishop, pondering the "one bullet" puzzle, concluded: "I believe Roy [Brown] let go pretty much all over the sky, probably while skidding, and that Richthofen was so unfortunate (from his point of view) as to fly directly into the path of one bullet. That is infinitely more likely to be what happened than that a man on the ground fired one shot from a rifle and performed one of the greatest single feats of the war."[29]

Bishop's views offered an odd sort of support for Brown and machine guns: in short, Brown was inept, but lucky. Perhaps.

Another explanation for low bullet density consists of bullet scatter, or spread, resulting when firing a machine gun from an aircraft. For some examples, see the shot patterns of chapter 2. A practical summing up of Camel shot group possibilities at a reasonable range was given by Orfordness machine gun experts: "in the hands of experienced people . . . it is possible to put 70 to 80% of the shots into a 20 ft. circle enclosing the target on good days, but on bad days the bullets may spread out over 100 ft. or more."[30]

As used here, "good" or "bad" refers to air turbulence level, with "good" meaning low turbulence.

A "good day" drawing, to scale, of Richthofen's Dr. I

The Single Bullet Puzzle

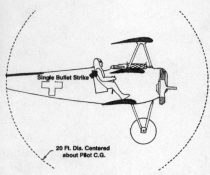

20 Ft. Dia. Centered
about Pilot C.G.

Single Bullet Strike

(left) Rhinebeck's air show replica Fokker Triplane offers us a gunner's view of Richthofen's end; (right) with the single, fatal bullet entering through his right arm pit. The large circle represents the perimeter of bullet scatter to be expected from a Camel's guns on a calm day. Sources: (left) original photo; (right) original drawing from data, chapter 8, note 30.

fuselage with a 20-foot circle superimposed, circled about the sitting pilot's C.G. (his belly button), shows the arena that most fired bullets traversed. If we imagine Brown, a bit excited, extending the usual five-round burst to ten, some seven or eight bullets would pass through the circular perimeter shown. The area is large (314 square feet). It's not difficult to picture eight rounds distributed within, of which only one struck Richthofen, with the other seven missing the engine.

In short, a Camel-fired Vickers burst hitting Richthofen with only one bullet is not surprising. It isn't necessary to bring in Bishop's shooting-while-skidding premise to explain the one-bullet result. Finally, if the day is considered less "good"—and all accounts term it a windy and gusty day typical of April—the resulting shot scatter circle would be that much larger, until we are surprised that even one bullet struck Richthofen.

In contrast, ground-based machine-gun fire produces a much tighter pattern. See chapter 2. Mounted on a light tripod, and firing at a great range of 660 yards, a Vickers machine gun was able to put 83 percent of its bullets into a 21 square foot target; an area much smaller—a tiny 7 percent or so—of the comparable airborne figure given above. At the short ranges claimed by the Australian gunners, still tighter patterns would be expected.

Why this huge difference between ground- and air-fired shot scatter?

There were two reasons: support stiffness and air turbulence. A ground mounted gun using a properly set tripod offered support rigidity greatly exceeding that offered by a light and unstable aircraft. Secondly, air turbulence serving to disturb and alter aircraft path, greatly altering airborne gun alignment, had little influence upon ground-fired guns.

In use against a crossing target, ground guns must pivot slightly in order to maintain lead. The resulting pattern opens somewhat, but all the bullets within a burst hit close to their aiming point. Scatter remains small.

Thus the one bullet premise raises doubts about the case of the Australian machine gunners. We anticipate ground-based shot groups to be tight, implying that if any one bullet hit, more should have followed.

In short, machine-gun shot pattern considerations point to Brown as a better bet than the Australians. What of the rifleman? Were his chances as unlikely as Bishop would have it?

Bishop's contempt for the rifleman possibility was contradicted by the theoretical calculations of A. Mallock. He determined an expert rifleman's chance for placing a bullet within a passing aircraft's vital 20 square feet to be about one in eight. His shooter was assumed to be at an optimum range and acquainted with the proper lead for a 100 MPH machine.[31] In reality, shooters were rarely so well favored, usually knowing little of the speed or lead to be employed against crossing aircraft. Even so, the rifleman prospect can't be dismissed. Too many combat fliers were downed by hits registered under similar conditions. Although overly optimistic, something like Mallock's odds remain creditable. As for precisely how creditable, we can't judge; unless the single bullet premise itself is shot down, an unknown rifleman as victor over Richthofen remains a serious possibility.

Two battles involving Richthofen have been examined. They tell us something of the interplay between chance, tactics, and technology. In the first, tactics set the rules, with aircraft design dealing the cards. Skill level was high but limited to only one test: flying in the tightest circle possible with the least possible loss of height. Late in the game, Richthofen won as a result of his opponent's malfunctioning engine, with his own good shooting an important secondary factor.

In Richthofen's last battle, the level of confusion remains too high to reach any verdict. He was shot dead by a single bullet emerging from an airborne machine gun, or possibly a ground-based machine gun, or even an infantry rifle. Of these three possibilities the odds, based on shot scatter analysis, don't favor the claims of ground-based machine gunners. Either Brown or the unknown rifleman appear more probable as victors.

Was it all luck? Or if not quite all, then mostly luck? If Hawker's engine had performed properly, it's possible that Richthofen would have fallen and not Hawker. Luck obviously had a strong impact on the result. As for the uncertainty surrounding Richthofen's end, the very concept of bullet scatter is one that embraces luck and attempts to subdue it—a business of transforming chance into something better than mere shoulder shrugging. With luck or chance so strongly featured as a decision maker, consider this extreme possibility: aces accumulating vast numbers of air combat victories did so entirely as a result of luck.

For justification, we might reason that the competing machines were usually fairly evenly matched and, given some minimum of experience, pilots achieved roughly equal skills. With all seemingly equal, was luck the only uncertainty?

To test the power of luck, imagine combat to consist of a two-person game, much like drawing for high cards where depending upon the card drawn one person wins and his opponent loses. Imagine the game to be conducted honestly, with skill having nothing to do with the results, and each loser continually replaced by a fresh entrant. What are the chances that any one player can achieve eighty consecutive victories? The answer is: less than one chance in a thousand billion times a thousand billion.[32] A probability this small is negligible—in the real world, it wouldn't happen. The existence of other high victory scores in the 70s and 60s confirm the unlikelihood of such an event arising through chance. Nature might permit one such high score to pass as a freak happening—but not a handful.

Returning to our premise—no, it wasn't luck, certainly not in the case of very high scores. What about low scores? Using the same card game assumptions, the chances of ten victories in a row are reckoned to be about one in a thousand.[33] This number has some bite; we are approaching reality. For five consecutive victories, the odds are about one in thirty-two.[34] That one fits everyday reality. Given many hundreds of fighter pilots, it's almost certain that some became aces—that is, achieved 5 victories—through luck alone.

In short, luck counted, especially at the beginning of a fighting career when all was ignorance. As experience built up, judgment entered the picture, becoming crucial as scores mounted. In the matter of Hawker versus Richthofen, Hawker's failure was largely one of judgment. He knew his engine to be a lemon. He knew that even if it performed perfectly, his aircraft was unable to either out-speed or dive away from his opponent. Yet he entered combat voluntarily as an aggressor, though lacking any genuine need to do so. Here was a brave man, one refusing to consider the odds.

A certain heedless quality may well be the true measure of heroism. The difficulty comes in separating such selfless behavior from stupidity. If somehow each man had been given the opposing machine to fly, Richthofen, a strong believer in the odds, would likely have refused combat. Logic was his strength. Unlike the Red Baron, Hawker drew strength from his support of management's stirring philosophy: attack at all cost! Unfortunately for Hawker, the gods of combat preferred logic to drama, and so he died.

Not all fighter pilot effort went into chasing victories. Many more might have been achieved, but oddly enough, some victories were unwanted . . .

9

Unwanted Victories

AIR COMBAT MEMOIRS REPORT AN UNRE-
lenting pressure for victories, with acceptance as a man and
prestige as a warrior dependent upon one's numerical
standing. As fliers saw it, the pressure was limited only by
accident or death. In reality there were other constraints:
some pilots were too important to lose in combat and, to
a fussy management, some victories were of the wrong kind.
A need for instructors with current experience resulted in
the curtailing of frontline victories for many gifted shooters. Transfers to inactive fronts reduced others to mere
spear holders. Although injuries and death obviously
played a large part, the greatest limit to victory number
was posed by success itself—the greater the success, the
more likely some form of official restriction would arise,
cutting off further victories.

In acting to limit personal victories for the top aces,
management had mixed motives. Humane considerations
were part of the picture, for those who had done more
than their share were entitled to a reprieve from war. It was
also useful to have proven fighting men available as con-
sultants and administrators, greatly improving the level of
war planning. Finally, top aces made superb icons, suited
for employment in rock star fashion as recruiting draws or
public relations glad-handers.

How many victories were enough? First, how many victories might have been expected? With hundreds of men in
the RFC and German Air Service qualifying as aces, how
many victories could be reasonably expected from the top
scorers? Was Richthofen's count of eighty a good enough
performance—or were many more possible?

Consider the act of competitive achievement itself. Whether the goal is one of writing scientific papers for a sharply critical audience or shooting down airplanes, the same laws apply—the greater the performance, the fewer the able practitioners. We know this from sports experience; many men can hit a few home runs, but very few can hit fifty per season.

The basic rule—Lotka's Law—is given on page 167 portraying the relative output of technical article writers.[1] Shown is a plot of the number of articles produced per writer—ranging from one to ten—against the number of writers achieving that particular level of productivity. As the output (articles per author) becomes greater, fewer authors (y-axis) are capable of shouldering the burden.

Applying Lotka's Law: the number of capable writers go as 100 divided by the square of author's published articles. For example, if we have one hundred writers capable of turning out one article in some period of time, how many authors are capable of turning out ten articles in the same time? If we take 10 and square it, we have 100. Dividing into 100, the answer is 1; or, only one author exists capable of generating ten times as much useful work as the typical one-article writer.

The law has been checked and tested with published scientific output and holds up well indeed. The particular form of plot used here, the log-log, has the advantage of displaying power law terms (that business of squaring, or cubing, etc.) in a straight-line format, making it a bit easier to extend the curve into uncharted waters.[2] There is a drawback in the form of nonlinear x and y scales—certainly annoying when positioning data points—but as prices go, it seems a reasonable one to pay in return for straight-line results.

Although we must grant Lotka credit for nailing down an elusive truth, common sense questions the craft of article writing as analogous to air combat. Article writers aren't shot dead for making a mistake, and so go on endlessly, ceasing only when in the grave. A more realistic model might employ pitching for a major league baseball team. Here injury, age, and fatigue play an important role, ending the working life of players. Throwing enough mistakes yields, if not death, then a sure ticket to oblivion. In statistical terms, there is no difference, for those who are either dead or transported to the minors no longer appear on the roster.

For data, we employ major league results of lifetime

pitching performance taken from the first four hundred ace pitchers (five victories or more) as listed alphabetically (A to middle C).[3] Plotting 400 points, containing many duplicates, can result in a messy presentation. For clarity, registers have been used. For example, all 129 pitchers winning between five and nineteen games are plotted as a single horizontal band; ditto all sixty-four victories over the range twenty to thirty-four. Real points (round, filled) are employed only when the top scorers emerge, and are shown on the horizontal axis. These represent the lifetime efforts of Steve N. Carlton (329 wins) and Grover C. Alexander (373).

The results ('Baseball Pitcher Victory Frequency,' p. 168) differ from those based on article writers in one important respect: pitcher output consists of a broken line rather a simple straight one. Somewhere near eighty lifetime victories, the curve breaks, meaning that additional victories are that much more difficult to come by. Those able to pay the steep price for eighty-plus victories were few. In short, something dramatic occurs in the eighty-plus neighborhood—what?

Old age comes early to pitchers. Achieving eighty victories takes many years of effort. By then the pitcher is old, if not in the conventional sense, then by the standards of cumulative muscle strain and fatigue. Managers and owners know this, plan on it, and act without mercy when the time comes and the pitcher weakens. That sharp break in the victory curve signifies the disappearance of peers and the rarity of further victories.

Some men struggle on, and the trend line points to roughly 250 victories as a reasonable expectation for the highest scorer. Greatly exceeding this number, Carlton and Alexander demonstrated truly extraordinary performance. Whether their winning records reflected canniness, a dead ball, batter inability to hit a curve, or the sly use of spitballs is best left to others.

What can be said of our procedure? Given enough performance data, leading performer output can be projected, if we are satisfied with a rough estimate. It's then possible to find and credit those few who greatly exceed reasonable expectations—those either craftier or more skillful than their peers and so able to press on after their competitors have faded. Finally, it's possible to use the slope of output versus number of performers curves to gauge the level of difficulty encountered—the greater the slope or falloff, the greater the difficulty. However, rather than make slope

Article Writing Frequency
(number of authors writing given number of articles)

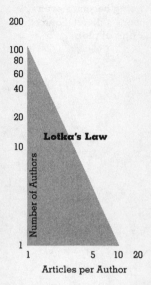

Lotka's Law plot shows the ultra-achiever to be a rare bird. Only one writer in a hundred puts out ten times as much product as the ordinary author. *Source:* original plot, heavily influenced by similar graph, chapter 9, note 1.

Baseball Pitcher Victory Frequency

Winning pitching differs from article writing in one important respect: after eighty wins, the going becomes even more difficult. *Source: original plot.*

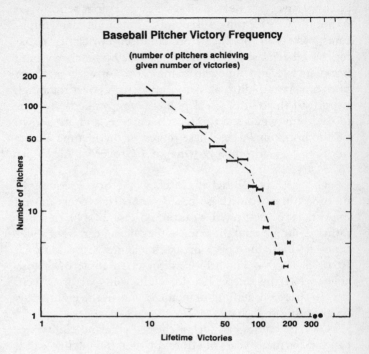

Baseball Pitcher Victory Frequency

(number of pitchers achieving given number of victories)

measurements, we'll be satisfied with an eyeball judgment—"more difficult" or "less difficult" will do.

Turning to German Air Service records to examine frequency of success ('German Victory Frequency,' p. 169) we again employ registers spanning a range of victories.[4] Our tabulation has been handled in the same manner as the baseball results. For example, all 216 pilots accredited with between five to nine victories are presented by a single band, for otherwise the heavy duplication would muddy the waters and interfere with trend spotting. Again, top scorers are represented by round, filled points located on the x-axis. These stand for: Ltn. Erich Lowenhardt (54), Ltn. Ernst Udet (62), and Rittmeister Manfred von Richthofen (80).

The results consist of a broken line, with a new, more difficult slope starting at about the forty-victory level. Let's examine the full output curve, bit by bit, starting at the top. Upon becoming an ace, further victories proved difficult to attain, with a degree of difficulty about equal to those described by Lotka's inverse square law. For example, only one-quarter of all German aces were able to improve their score by doubling their victories (say from six to

German Victory Frequency

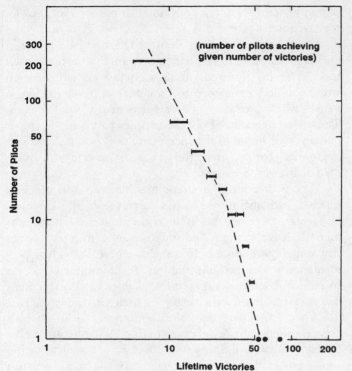

(number of pilots achieving given number of victories)

German aces found compiling more than forty victories to be especially difficult. *Source:* original plot.

twelve). In short, doubling wasn't easy, proving much more difficult than doubling early pitching victories (steeper slope).

At the forty-victory break point noted, matters became still more difficult (even greater slope). Moving toward the individual high scorers, victory data suggest a Lowenhardt/Udet average as a reasonable top score, with only Richthofen exceeding expectations. As the broken-line result is very much like that of winning pitcher frequency, we tend to blame the same root cause—aging. However, though the war may have seemed endless, few Great War pilots actually saw more than two years of combat and fewer still were engaged for more than three. With most pilots inducted in their teens or early twenties, it is difficult to credit the following two or three years of service, no matter how difficult, as having physically aged flying personnel to the point where further victories became less likely. If anything, skill and coordination usually improve with a few years of experience. As the usual victim was someone with only a slight knowledge of fighting, one might expect old-timer aces to find victories ever easier to score as their experience continued to mount. Yet the victory frequency plot shows this was not so. Why not?

If not aging itself, then combat fatigue was a factor in limiting victories by old hands. Although the term itself had yet to be invented, all air services watched for men who trembled, or needed too much alcohol, or made too many mistakes, or developed a permanent violent temper. These were transferred out, sometimes to a quiet front, or perhaps sent home to instruct a batch of truly unfortunate beginners—for no instructor was as bad as one who trembled at the very idea of flying.

Yet another limiting factor was burnout and its close relative—exhaustion owing to overwork. With a big push underway, there was no limit to the demands put on airmen. All leave was canceled and as many as four patrols per day somehow endured. In an area where individual performance was everything, the burden of endless work was too much. Even the youngest lost their edge. Management had no sympathy for the weary—if their victories were few.

When Lt. Albert Ball, already an ace and an obvious comer, requested a few days rest (July 1916) he was transferred out of a fighting unit and into an observation squadron—a clear slap in the face.[5] Management was not about to accept suggestions from nineteen-year-old boys, talented or not, and if overall victories suffered from curious transfers, so be it.

Another possibility leading to the broken-line result was a simple transfer of old hands to administrative functions. Noting that the break came at about the forty-victory point—the score of Ltn. Oswald Boelcke—we might reason that the German Air Service accepted the revered Boelcke's death with remorse, and set out to change matters. Uneasy at his persistence in flying routine combat missions, management fears were confirmed when Boelcke, a prized intellectual and ombudsman, died in a pointless collision with his wingman. The broken line suggests an administrative move to prevent recurrence—by loading old hands with many noncombat duties, risk was reduced, at the price of lost scoring opportunities.

Richthofen accepted this explanation. As he put it, "I had been allowed to bag only 41. Anyone will be able to guess why."[6]

Was the forty-victory break uniquely German? Were all

British Victory Frequency

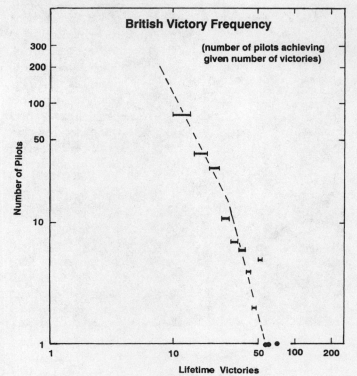

British Victory Frequency

(number of pilots achieving given number of victories)

Number of Pilots

Lifetime Victories

British victory trends were identical to the German. Both are represented by the same (traced) broken line result. *Source:* original plot.

ace victory counts much alike, regardless of service? A plot of British victory frequency shows a surprising similarity.[7] Indeed, the dashed result has been traced from the plot of German results. Observation shows the fit to the British data to be good. So long as we confine our efforts to rough estimates there is no difference between British and German frequency of victories. Each reveals the same broken-line output with a break point in the vicinity of forty victories. In other words, ace pilots in each service experienced equal difficulty in compiling victories, and those conquests gained after a count of forty or so were more difficult to come by than those before. Top scores were those of Maj. Edward Mannock (61), Maj. Raymond Collishaw (62), and Maj. William A. Bishop (72).

In short, the prospects for victory accumulation by British and German aces were interchangeable. How did this curious similarity come about? Didn't differences in technology count? Were victories primarily a matter of

Ltn. Oswald Boelcke

His accidental death after reaching forty victories influenced German thinking; acting to curtail combat for other high scorers. *Source:* Sanke Photo Studio, Berlin, 1916.

chance, with luck shared equally by both services and the resulting identical victory frequency a mathematical certainty?

One believer was Lt. Arthur Rhys-Davids (25) who argued, "Except for one's first half dozen scraps it's largely a question of luck—stray bullets."[8] To the truly skilled, the factor of luck (the first sighting of an enemy, wind direction, jammed guns, etc.) was infuriating; at times luck served to swamp the value of hard-earned skill. Indeed, sometimes luck ruled, but the very existence of high-scoring aces proved that much more than luck was involved, for no man is always lucky, and the ability of leading aces to win many dozens of encounters despite frequent bad cards required enormous skill.

Luck alone wasn't the answer. Rhys-Davids's view was extreme, and smacked of despair. Skill, technology, strategy, and personnel policy were all highly pertinent to victory frequency. Equality of victory frequency meant equality of the total influence of these factors, that is, the summed total of (skill + luck + technology + strategy + personnel policy) for each side was equal.

Of these factors, personnel policy may well have had the strongest influence. Consider the views of Lt. Ball in a letter to his girlfriend Flora (April 1917): "My total is now 34. Only three more to get before I am top of England and France again. In order to whack the German man (Boelcke) [*sic*] I have got about ten more to get. If it's God's will that I should do it then I will come home."[9]

Ball was convinced that beating Boelcke's record meant a ticket home and assignment to noncombat duty. If so, any further victories would be greatly delayed, assuring a falloff of high score victories. The observed break in the victory frequency curve is an exact fit to such a process. Ball's scheme would explain a great deal—but did the "Boelcke victory break" really exist, or was it a despairing young man's pie-in-the-sky dream?

Ball himself never completed his own quota of victories. He was dead within a month, leaving his plan unfulfilled. An examination of the lives of other top aces is illuminating.

In July 1918, having achieved exactly forty victories, Ltn. Ernst Udet was given one month of home leave; time spent dictating his memoirs and helping judge the winner of a fighter plane competition.[10] The value of these activities were slight when assessed in comparison with Germany's last-gasp drive on Paris, occurring simultaneously. As given by German Chancellor von Hertling: "We expected grave events in Paris for the end of July [1918]. That was on the 15th. On the 18th even the most optimistic among us understood that all was lost."[11]

So great was Germany's commitment to the forty-victory break that Udet was sent off to fritter away a month despite the obvious, desperate need for every major player. Should a month off seem a slender respite from death, Germany's needs could yield only small reprieves. Richthofen, unable to tear himself away in the midst of Bloody April (1917) saw his victory count mount from thirty-two to fifty-two.[12] Finally able to break away in May, he enjoyed a hero's leave complete with boar hunting and the dictation of memoirs.[13] By mid-June he was back at work. Germany couldn't afford to do without his services for long. Management did reduce his combat load and encourage him to spend time as an unofficial inspector-general of fighter planes, in the manner of Boelcke. This he seized upon, and monitored the activities of an advanced flight school (Valenciennes), toured aircraft manufacturing plants, and politicked for a triplane fighter.[14] He even attended certain of the Russian surrender talks at Brest-Litovsk, adding glamour to an otherwise all political affair.[15] The net effect was to decrease his combat hours, a step taken to keep him alive and immediately available for any emergency—a compromise between grounding and full combat duty. As with most compromises, there were drawbacks, for it supplied neither true safety nor maximum victories. He died (April 1918) with eighty victories, certainly enough for any man, but there might have been many more.

The British were more willing to grant a complete change of duty. When top scorer Bishop reached the level of forty-seven victories (August 1917) he was ordered to his native Canada to serve as part of a recruiting campaign.[16] He returned to Britain as a gunnery school administrator enjoying a safe, quiet life until, becoming bored, he sought combat again. In all, he was away for nearly nine months. Collishaw, after thirty-eight victories (July 1917) involving at least one serious crash of his own, was also ordered off to Canada, not returning to action until year's end.[17] Once back, he was as effective as ever. Although the half-year rest obviously cut his victory total, he was well satisfied with the newly founded RAF and his final score of sixty, reenlisting after the war.

Some men did not welcome the forty-victory break. One was Maj. James B. McCudden, finally relieved (March 1918) after fifty-seven victories, mostly on SE5a fighters. McCudden's strange attitude toward combat was carefully summed by a sympathetic biographer: "his hopes of reaching von Richthofen's score were approaching obsessional state . . . he was developing a mild form of combat fatigue."[18] Only a troubled man would reject the gift of a well-earned rest in the hope of making it into the record books. Such was McCudden.

Most aces welcomed the break, long or short, and happily enjoyed whichever junket came their way—be it one to Canada or Berlin. As for personal scores, aces tended to have aggressive, competitive personalities, and likely regretted those victories missed owing to time off. Proof is contained in the numerous determined quests for a second tour of active duty. For example, that of McCudden, developed below.

How many victories were passed up? By canceling the transfers of all those released from active duty late in their careers, and forcing old hands to continue combat operations without a break, an estimate of additional virtual victories can be prepared. The necessary administrative action is simulated by extending the upper portion of the victory frequency line until it cuts the horizontal axis, as in 'British or German Victory Frequency,' p 176. The answer for the maximum number of projected personal victories—in either service—is about 120. Our conclusion: if set the task of combat without relief, the top ace's anticipated score, either British or German, would approximate 120 victories.

Neither side attempted such a policy, partly because it was too harsh. Bitter logic entered too, for in the aftermath of Boelcke's death, offering up the life of a knowledgeable fighting man in exchange for a few dozen enemy beginners seemed a poor trade. Old hands were pure gold, able to tell a good plane from bad, a good tactic from a stupid one, and a shrewd strategy from the hopeless "kill-em-all" desires of the public. In the real world of 1915–18 air combat there were too many hapless beginners, poorly trained and offering little threat to anyone other than themselves and their fellows. Some had only 15 hours of solo flight— these were pilots barely able to fly, much less fight.[19] To expend the lives of old timers in accidents incidental to the liquidation of enemy airmen was a winning game only if the losers had some merit. Indeed, this is the working assumption behind fighter victory scores: the score is, if not everything, then nearly everything. Management had come to know better. Blasting an endless supply of beginners did build scores, but scores were merely one of many things that mattered.

Old-timer aces mattered. They could step into top administrative jobs or act as key advisors. Without them, the war would go badly. When necessary, they could be returned to frontline duty. Unlike baseball pitchers, old aces never lost their mastery. Given some time to acclimate themselves, they proved as good as ever.

All in all, there was much logic behind management's decision to offer extended furlough or multiple mini-leaves to old-timer aces. As for the down side—fewer total victories—these were viewed as a relatively minor factor. One need not be a cynic to reason that wars are won by live, shrewd, battle-hardened planners, and not by body counts of ignorant beginners.

What of stress? Didn't combat stress slowly build up in each pilot, ultimately leading to combat fatigue? Wasn't it necessary to cut off further combat at some point, perhaps at forty victories, because no ordinary man could handle still higher levels of stress accumulation?

British or German Victory Frequency

Extending the upper por-
tion of the victory fre-
quency curve simulates
a 'no relief' policy leading to more victories.
Source: original plot.

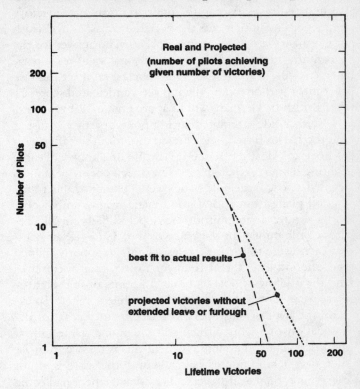

At the time, little was known of stress. Not until World War II did the RAF learn that 15 percent of its airmen would break down no matter how light a stress was applied, and another 15 percent would never crack no matter how severely stressed. The great mass of men in between (70 percent) were indeed sensitive to stress accumulation—there was much truth in the concept of accumulated stress leading to a breaking point—for the average man.[20]

That said, we aren't dealing with the average man. Any man capable of reaching forty victories has been sorely tried. If capable of breaking down, he would have done so. True, some of the aces seem strange indeed, but by the crude standards of the time, they remained effective, if not wholly sound. While it's impossible to predict the status of their psyche if pushed to further achievement without hope of relief, these men appear to be members of the impervious 15 percent. We believe them capable of many more victories than were achieved.

In sum: the broken-line victory frequency curve reflected decisions by the British and German higher command to foster survival of old-timer aces—the fittest of them all. Here were decisions in tune with nature itself. As guides go, it's difficult to find a better one.

Many old-timer aces were not content with their peaceful, kept-on-ice assignments. It wasn't easy to switch from combat to instruction. To serve as recruiting icons made many men feel foolish. Those hooked on kill-or-be killed hunting found posing for patriotic postcards a silly business. The desire to return to combat was strong, and in the case of McCudden there was considerable logic behind the wish. He hoped to return as leader of a new concept—defensive air warfare.

The land war was a bad war. Static war in muddy trenches proved difficult to accept. To the public, it didn't seem a proper war. The importance of poison gas and heavy cannons devalued individual fighting men. Bravery or initiative counted for little; the resulting casualties were too large to be grasped.

In refreshing contrast, the fighter pilot as aerial duelist proved enormously successful with the public. Here was war as it should be, with each nation's gladiators fighting it out against a blue sky. Skill and daring counted. Casualties were few. There were even aces whose exploits could be followed, much as in sports.

The flaw was one of uncertain significance, for the war was undeniably a land war at core. The views of top infantry officers were crucial and spending much energy to liquidate enemy fighter pilots seemed wrong to infantry officers. What counted was the elimination of enemy machines carrying out reconnaissance and strafing missions, that is, wiping out the "working machines!" Instead, RFC /RAF fighter pilots, if given a choice, attacked opposing fighter pilots, automatically gunning for their most dangerous enemies. The difficulty with the resulting fracas was that it usually left working machines unharmed. In early 1918, anxious infantry lobbyist Colonel Repington complained, "The increase in air fighting is affecting the execution of really serious work"—a polite way of putting down air combat itself while criticizing the air service for mistaken priorities.[21]

McCudden was that rare fighter pilot who specialized in bringing down working machines: those two-seaters charged with photography, artillery ranging, bombing, or contact patrol efforts (trench strafing). Of these, the high altitude reconnaissance plane was his favored opponent. Equipped with the personality of a perfectionist loner and gifted with a feeling for machinery, he found the painstaking pursuit of a single two-seater enemy to his liking. Content to spend half an hour or more easing his lone SE5a into a good firing position, he fought a slow-motion war using stealth instead of aerobatics.

There were limits to his patience. Bored with a post-combat assignment as instructor, he sensed that something had changed when the aeronautical press admitted: "Unfortunately, it has become the habit for fighting machines to seek out other fighting machines rather than to chase working machines . . . the true duties of the fighting machine have of late been forgotten."[22]

If from Repington, the statement would have been dismissed as more of the usual infantry grousing; but the source was C. G. Grey, an air power extremist and journalist of the most partisan type. McCudden felt that his time had come. He prepared "a scheme" (May 1918) and sent it along, through channels, to the highest-ranking RAF officers. His views received careful attention at every stage, finally yielding a considered response from the RAF's commanding officer, given below.[23]

McCudden opened by declaring his goal: the denial of valuable intelligence to the enemy, intelligence gathered by two-seater aircraft. All reconnaissance missions could be divided into (A) low altitude work close to the lines, (B) medium altitude flights (6,000 to 16,000 feet) with about 5 to 30 minutes of intrusion over British lines, and (C) high altitude observation (16,000 to 23,000 feet) with from 30 minutes to 2 hours of intrusion. At the moment "our own aerial work is purely offensive and we have no system whereby we interrupt or disorganize this important aerial activity on the enemy's part."

To destroy all intruders was impractical, but he believed a zone some 40 miles wide could be kept clear by a squadron of picked pilots consisting of six to twelve men, chosen as "skillful, not in the least offensively reckless, and above all patient." As for their aircraft, the necessary qualities were "climb, speed, forward, and upward view. Maneuverability and stability does not so much matter . . . Vickers guns only. Suitable machines: SE5a fitted with either H.C. 200 or 300 HP Hispano . . . [four other possibilities were listed]."

As for the officer in charge of this squadron, he lightly

touched on his own superb credentials: "What success I had in France was not my flying, or shooting, but simply through thoroughly studying the habits of the enemy."[24]

One possible drawback to victory was noted: the enemy might react to attack by escorting his two-seaters. As McCudden saw it, such an attempt must fail, for the Germans had no scout able to match the brilliant performance of their Rumplers—that is, the escorts couldn't keep up.

To modern eyes, the concept seems plausible but the proposal lacks details and the project appears understaffed. Many bureaucratic objections would seem in order. The actual response was quite different.

Maj. Gen. J. M. Salmond, Commanding RAF HQ, In the Field, had recently succeeded Maj. Gen. Hugo M. Trenchard. A dominant personality, Trenchard was known for his emphatic belief in an offensive posture at all times, with fighting limited to the enemy's air space.[25] Salmond's views on defensive interception were little known. An instructor initially, he rose to the highest field rank, not as an initiator but as an efficient administrator.[26]

In response to McCudden, Salmond wrote, "For a limited period the suggested tactics would be successful . . . however the enemy is not deterred by opposition. The result of bringing down those high flyers, which fly singly, would be they would be sent over in formation . . . the few specially trained pilots would be unable to tackle them . . . the result would be more hostile machines over our lines than is the case at present . . . the offensive-defensive attitude . . . is, to my mind, unsound and should neither be taught nor encouraged."[27]

In short, the McCudden approach was viewed as a mistaken concept. Whatever victories might be achieved through interception were unwanted, for German losses would merely force a change of enemy tactics, leading to still greater British vulnerability.

Like Trenchard, Salmond was quite willing to wage aggressive war, and those victories gained over enemy turf were greatly desired. However, victories over British-held turf were not. Defeatism wears many faces. Salmond's defeatism was that of a weary trench warrior refusing to face any additional problem—"Let's not do anything about that enemy mortar, because if we knock it out, they'll just put two mortars on us." An understandable attitude, certainly human, but no way to win a war.

McCudden was soon killed in a flying accident. Always a loner, he left no disciples to carry on his winning, though detested, form of aerial warfare. In any list of unwanted victories, those of McCudden must be placed at the top. Was he somehow responsible for the rejection of his ideas?

Not really, though he was not the best of advocates. He was born on the wrong side of the tracks. He was a technical specialist when the classical scholar ruled. He didn't mix well. As an air combat leader he had too many victories, as compared to those of his peers. His victims fell behind British lines and so could be easily counted—his victories were real. Envious competitors fought over German turf with uncertain success, despite official assurance that all was well. He was loud and clear and deferred to no man—not even mechanics. He thought well of himself and made it clear that he did so.

He was that rare know-it-all who happened to be right. No system welcomes such a man. However, the system was sufficiently sophisticated to distinguish between man and message. It was the message that was rejected, partly because it offered support for the infantry, but mostly because of the failure of prior aerial blockades. Spirited aggressors were believed to be more than a match for the usual sluggish defense and the French failure to keep the skies clear of Germans over Verdun convinced Trenchard that interception was a hopeless business. As for McCudden's proven success, it was judged to be merely a fluke. With interception not on the table, McCudden's proposal had no chance, for each of his victories was a blow to higher command's basic philosophy.

The Germans also viewed certain victories as undesirable— those resulting from combat on the British side of the line. Initially this restraint came from the desire to protect against the loss of technical secrets built into Fokker's synchronized machine gun, a restriction reflecting common sense. However, the geographical curfew continued long after an unlucky German ferry pilot, lost on a foggy day, delivered a spanking new E-III to the Allies, complete with a synchronized machine gun.[28] Despite the loss of secrecy, German fighter pilots continued their reluctance to fight over British-held turf unless participating in a major offensive. Much as British pilots were encouraged to fight well outside their lines—in precisely opposite fashion—German pilots were discouraged from fighting beyond their own lines.

To an extent, the German concept employed good tactical reasoning. To fight over one's own turf meant that a

French Defense Failure

Original (1917) German caption: "A French aircraft shot down over Verdun." Failure of French all-out local air defense efforts discouraged similar British "blockades." Source: Baer, ed., Der Volkerkrieg, vol. 14, 128.

forced landing was without risk of capture—an important consideration at a time when all fighter planes had bugs, when even the best engines were rated at only 150 hours between major overhauls, and the worst (rotaries) were good for 60 hours, if that. The Albatros fighter series, and the Nieuport series as well, suffered wing failure if dived too fast. Guns were notorious for their jamming tendencies. Knowing the inadequacies of their equipment only too well, it's understandable that pilots preferred to fight close to home.

Even so, in accepting the front lines as a barrier, the Germans abandoned many low-risk scoring opportunities. Badly shot up British machines—easy victims—weren't pursued over the lines. The many tossed-away victories suggest more than tactical prudence. Deeper strategic issues were involved.

Paramount was Germany's limited strength when measured against that of the Allies. Coincident with the extraordinary German fighter success of Bloody April (1917) came the U.S. entrance into the war, a grim indicator of future Allied power. To a Germany barely capable of containing the pre-U.S. Allies, future fighter hopes could not be based on the aggressive many, as were British plans, but were limited to the actions of a gifted few. These were to fight defensively to husband their strength while offering maximum punishment to the Allies. Then, whenever desired, German fighter pilots could be delivered to any portion of the front in large numbers, using a traveling circus concept to outnumber and destroy local opposition.

Richthofen's experience was a perfect fit. Fighting over his own turf, he was forced down with a broken wing and separately, was shot down by a lucky gunner. In each case, an equivalent RFC pilot would have served out the war as a prisoner. By fighting on his side of the line he was able to experience, if not nine lives, then certainly many more than one.

Germany, like Britain, had its unwanted victories. Building scores was all very well, but each side had higher goals. As a result, no man achieved the 120 victories shown possible.

In sum: personal victories under forty in number were welcomed by every air service. However, those over forty were accepted reluctantly, for each additional victory implied excessive risk for an obviously valuable fighting man. Other unwanted victories were those regarded as wrong in principle: for the British, these included the results of high altitude interception over British-held turf; for the Germans, those gained on the British side of the lines.

Although victories were obviously useful, other considerations set limits, preventing any pilot from reaching an estimated theoretical peak of 120 victories.

Udet Summary by Udet

"I've had sixty-two victories and sixty-two years of life. The victories were the best part." The strain of serving as a German General directly under Goering in World War II, added to the struggle against his own womanizing and alcoholic traits, led Udet to suicide at age forty-five. *Source:* Udet, *Hals und Beinbruch,* unpaged introduction. Drawings not retouched, but captions translated and updated.

Conclusions

Bullets as Menace

Prewar concern over the susceptibility of scout aircraft to marksman's bullets led to British field tests, with a large towed kite standing in for the airplane. Whether fired from ground-based rifle or machine guns, only one in two hundred bullets hit home, convincing top brass that bullet threat to aircraft, while significant, was minor. No sensible pilot would hang about, waiting for two hundred incoming bullets. More worrisome were accidents owing to pilot error and factory defects.

Wartime experience led to a greatly revised view of the expert shooter's chances. If given great skill, the right range, and a precise knowledge of the target aircraft's speed, the likelihood of a rifleman's hit in a vital spot was computed to be one in eight—a useful balance for the prewar figure, with the truth somewhere between.

Air Combat Weapons

To optimize the shooter's chances, the right weapon was crucial. For aircraft-to-aircraft combat, pistols, carbines, rifles, machine guns, mortars, and cannons were investigated. Each had major drawbacks. The machine gun, though it prevailed, was subject to jamming and reloading problems. With pilots experiencing serious jams at an average rate of once per month, repairs in flight were a must. Gun positions remote from the pilot made repair/reloading efforts that much more difficult and yet could offer a tactical gain—for example, the ability of pull-down guns to shoot upward—a tactical gain found important by leading aces Ball and Bishop.

Gun Jams

The type of machine gun, Vickers or Lewis, made little difference to jamming rate. Those pilots who reasoned that carrying one of each type would assure at least one functioning gun at all times, learned to their sorrow that if one jammed the other would likely follow—testifying to the role of freezing cloud moisture or rain in causing jams.

Aim Correction

The two great error sources in aerial shooting were those of gravity drop (elevation) and target motion (lead or deflection). Elevation correction had a lengthy history, drawing upon centuries of hunting experience. Deflection was a new and much greater problem, with proper aiming requiring as much as ten times the offset employed for elevation.

Tracers

Seemingly the answer to the problem of accuracy, tracers proved largely useless. An early hope was to adjust the tracer trajectory until it coincided with that of the target. However, combat reality showed something to be amiss. The four drawbacks and illusions present in tracer employment were: false hits, old news, false center of aim, and false trajectory. British tracer studies ended in despair, with gunners instructed to disregard tracer indications as misleading.

Gun Sights and Accuracy

Good shooting required knowledge of the enemy range, velocity, and direction. Early iron sights offered little help in making the necessary judgments. Given only a split second for deliberation, it wasn't easy to decide whether one's opponent was flying in a normal, high-speed attitude or in a yawed (crabbed) near-stalling position. Yet any misjudgment could be ruinous. Even with accurate input, early sights required precise eye location at the sight, not easy to achieve when faced with turbulence, gun vibration, and impatience.

Development efforts slowly improved gun sight accuracy. The Aldis optical sight eliminated the need for precise head positioning. Vane and gear sights compensated for flexible gun positioning. Turret mounting of twin guns became practical. With better engine performance and improved sights, tactics altered, for example, the offset or pull-down gun faded away. Yet despite significant improvements in precision, few men could shoot accurately over longer ranges—at 250 yards or more. For most, the only certain way of downing an enemy was to achieve a position immediately behind and fewer than 50 yards away—effectively eliminating the gun sight problem.

Performance

Fighter pilots wanted the best possible aircraft performance in the areas of maximum speed, rate of climb, maneuverability, and diving speed. Secondary but useful traits included the ability to carry heavy armor over a great range. These goals were largely antagonistic and priority of choice changed frequently as the nature of air war itself altered over time. As a further complication, Allied management pressed for simplicity of production, pursuing a late war plan to swamp their foes with many times the number of aircraft available to the Germans. To bring off this scheme it was necessary to settle for machines that were good enough, even if not the best—the SE5a and Camel. These had the virtue of equaling or bettering the performance of their most probable German opponents—the Albatros series of fighters—though they failed to match the best, for example, the Fokker D7F.

Wing Number

Biplane designs ruled. Triplane designs, pursued by both Sopwith and Fokker, were dropped as less than optimum. The British machine was perceived as too stable and "stately" in maneuver; the German version, though championed by the Red Baron, was ultimately phased out as inferior to the Fokker biplane (D7).

Vision

Needs were directed at seeing the opposing pilot first—a major combat advantage. One means of achieving this aim was to make oneself less visible. Experiments employing clear plastic coverings were attempted and failed; if anything, glancing sunlight emphasized existence. Improving one's vision through cutouts, relocating the pilot, wing stagger, and such, was widely employed in the hope of reducing the pilot blind angle—that sector in which an enemy might approach unseen. This process was effective, though it usually entailed a price in the form of reduced performance. Of the two late-war British fighters, the SE5a was much superior to the Camel in terms of blind angle.

Defensive Armor

Always an attractive prospect to aircrew, armor played little actual part owing to its tendency to reduce performance. With comprehensive protection requiring hundreds of pounds of metal plate, only the largest of engines could fly the resulting package, and the lack of maneuverability of the resulting machine was frightening to many pilots. What could be done at the practical level was to settle for small metal plates at strategically mounted locations, done at a low cost in weight. One 1916 British decision gave the pilot an armored seat; his gunner, nothing.

Red Baron Combat Analyzed

Detailed study of his lengthy circling fight with Hawker shows the importance of engine performance over a range of altitudes. Hawker initiated combat at a high altitude, one offering poor performance from his inferior engine, in the belief that more power, a tighter circle, and victory would follow as the fight wound downward to lower altitude. In reality his engine, a known lemon, did not develop the expected power bonus and he was killed in attempting to break out of the pursuit circle.

Death of the Red Baron

Possible claimants for the role of victor over Richthofen are examined in terms of ballistics, specifically bullet scatter and airborne dispersion studies. That one and only one round struck the Red Baron suggests a rifleman or a Camel fighter pilot as the more likely killer, when compared to a competent gunner equipped with a ground-based Vickers machine gun.

Unwanted Victories

At about the forty-victory level, German and British services imposed restraints limiting additional personal victories. Reasons ranged from the humanitarian to those of administrative needs, for high scorers had both precious expertise and value as icons too important to risk losing. Other unwanted victories were those regarded as wrong in principle: for the British, these included victories gained in defense, behind their lines at high altitude; for the Germans, those well behind the British lines. Had no restraint been in place, theoretical calculations indicate the maximum individual ace score might have approximated 120 victories.

Luck versus Skill

When examined with game theory, the belief that victory scores were primarily a matter of luck does receive support for low scores. In other words, it was quite possible to arrive at, say five victories, largely through luck. However, where high scores were concerned, luck is shown to be a minor factor as compared to skill and equipment. Assuming a rough balance of airplane design merit over the Western Front, those who achieved more than forty victories did so only through enormous skill and determination.

Glossary

AA or Archie.	Antiaircraft.
aileron.	Movable wing portion used to control roll.
Albatros.	Premier German aircraft manufacturer; products carried name.
Aldis sight.	Optical gun sight.
angle of attack.	Wing incidence corrected for downwash effect.
attitude.	Angular position of aircraft.
auto-rotation.	Forces initiating and extending spin.
azimuth.	Orientation in a left-right sense.
bank.	To tilt sideways; that is, to place one ear below the other.
BE2c.	British army cooperation aircraft; easy to fly, but a poor fighter.
BE12.	British fighter aircraft; unsuccessful in every respect.
Biggleswade, United Kingdom.	
	Location of Old Warden air museum and air shows.
biplane.	Aircraft with two wings.
Bloody April.	Period (1917) of huge British air losses.
breakaway.	Path used in fleeing or exiting from combat.
Bristol Scout.	Single-seater tractor, used in early war period.
Bristol F2b.	Two-seater tractor, successful as fighter in latter part war.
Camel.	British fighter aircraft; tricky, even treacherous, but successful.
castor oil.	Bean-derived lubricant especially suited for rotary engines.
Caudron GIV.	French two-seater, twin-engine machine, circa 1916.
cellon.	A form of celluloid used to cover aircraft.
ceiling.	Maximum operational altitude.
centrifugal force.	Outward force owing to curved motion.
C.G.	Center of gravity.
Clerget.	Well-regarded French-designed rotary engine, used by British.
click.	Smallest possible adjustment of aiming point.
CO or OC.	Commanding officer.
deflection.	Aim offset to allow for aircraft speed and attitude.
DH2.	British pusher fighter, useful in spring 1916, but quickly outdated.

DH4.	British bomber, highly successful.
DH5.	British fighter given negative stagger; unsuccessful, little used.
double.	Extra large drum of cartridges for Lewis gun, holding ninety-seven bullets.
dihedral.	Built-in upward angle of a wing toward its tips, front view.
dreidecker.	German term for triplane.
Dr. I.	Official German designation Fokker Triplane.
Dutch roll.	Aircraft lateral oscillation owing to instability.
E-III.	German fighter; revolutionary in 1915, outdated by late 1916.
elevation.	Vertical aim correction.
FE2b, FE2d.	British two-seater pusher fighter/bomber; successful.
FE8.	British single-seater pusher fighter, some limited success.
FK8.	British bomber aircraft.
fpm.	Climb rate in feet per minute.
flak.	Antiaircraft, German derivation.
flick.	Means of forcibly entering a spin.
FlugM.	(abb.). Flugmeisterei, German Air Intelligence.
Fokker D7.	Highly successful German single-seater fighter.
Fokker Triplane.	Three -winged single-seater fighter; limited success.
G loading.	Load factor compared to that of gravity.
G suit.	Garment opposing flow of body fluids when under acceleration.
gap/chord.	Ratio of the distance between wings to the wing breadth.
Gnome.	Brand of French rotary engines.
Gotha.	Manufacturer of German bombers.
gyroscopic force.	Force developed by rotating disc at right angle to load.
handy.	Easily maneuvered.
Hawker.	British aircraft manufacturer; for example, Hurricane. Unrelated to ace Lanoe Hawker.
Henri Farman.	French manufacturer of reconnaissance aircraft.
horn.	Aileron extension used for aerodynamic boost purposes.
HP.	(abb.). Horsepower.
IdFlieg.	(acronym). German Air Service.
incidence.	Angle between airfoil and oncoming air.
Jasta.	German Air Service unit designation.
Jenny.	Nickname U.S. trainer aircraft; JN4 to 6.
Kentucky windage.	Lead/deflection guesstimate.
lead.	Aim offset employed to compensate for target motion.
Lewis gun.	Light, drum-fed aircraft machine gun.
Lieut., Lt., Ltn.	(abb.). Lieutenant, respectively British, U.S., German.
Le Rhone.	French brand rotary engine, prized by German pilots.
line of sight.	Line between gunner's eye and target.
Lotka's Law.	Formula relating achievement to number of aspirants.
Luftwaffe.	German Air Service. IdFlieg was the older, prewar term.
LVG.	German manufacturer of two-seater observation and bombers.
Morane-Saulnier.	French manufacturer of successful two-seaters.

Mauser pistol.	German automatic; well regarded.
Mayfly.	British prewar dirigible; a failure.
Mercedes.	German stationary aircraft engine series, heavy but powerful.
Military Trials.	Prewar British competition for best military aircraft.
monoplane.	Airplane with a single wing.
Monosoupape.	French rotary engine, named for single valve operation.
NACA.	(abb.). National Advisory Committee for Aeronautics (USA).
NASA.	(abb.). National Aeronautics and Space Administration (USA).
NCO.	A noncommissioned officer.
Nieuport 11, 17.	Successful French single-seater fighters.
Norman sight.	Automatic sight, correcting for gunner's aircraft motion.
Oberursel.	German manufacturer of despised rotary engines.
One and 1/2 Strutter.	Successful British two-seater fighter, bomber.
Parabellum.	German flexible machine gun.
pitch.	Nose up or down change of attitude.
power loading.	Weight borne per horsepower.
prop.	Short for propeller.
Pup.	Sopwith fighter plane; maneuverable but underpowered.
pusher.	Aircraft with propeller at rear of fuselage.
P-40.	U.S. World War II fighter; sturdy but with mediocre maneuverability.
RAF.	(abb.). Royal Air Force; British Air Service. Also (abb.) Royal Aircraft Factory; official army aircraft manufacturer.
Red Baron.	German ace Manfred von Richthofen, a genuine baron who flew red-painted aircraft as a "come and get me" challenge.
RE8.	Widely used British army cooperation, bomber aircraft.
RFC.	(abb.). Royal Flying Corps, renamed RAF effective April 1918.
Rhinebeck, New York.	Site of Cole Palen's air show and museum.
roll.	Wing tip rotation; for example, roll to the left means left wing tip down.
Salamander.	Armored British single-seater; too heavy, too late.
Sanke.	German photo studio; many aces as customers.
SE5a.	Stable British fighter; successful. Employed latter part of war.
shrapnel.	AA shell load of small steel particles.
Siemens Schuckert SSW D4.	
	Promising German single-seater fighter.
Sopwith.	British aircraft manufacturer; a main source of fighters.
Sopwith Triplane	a.k.a. **Tripe.** Three-winged British single-seater fighter.
Sous-Lieut.	French rank, equivalent to Second Lieutenant.
SPAD 7, 13.	(abb.). Societe Pour l'Aviation et ses Derives; French aircraft manufacturer; fighters unusually sturdy and successful.
Spandau.	German belt-fed machine gun.
spiral dive.	Fast nose down dive along a path of large radius.
stab.	Stabilizer; part of horizontal tail; tends to promote stability.
staffel.	German Air Service unit designation.

stagger.	Fore and aft shift of lower wing chord relative to main wing in multiplane aircraft designs.
stall.	Breakaway of air flow from wing contour; can lead to spin trauma.
Storks.	Elite French fighter squadron.
synchronized gun.	Machine gun arranged to shoot between blades of revolving propeller.
Taube.	German observation aircraft used early in the war.
thrust.	Propeller output.
tractor.	Propeller in front of aircraft.
turning radius.	Measured aircraft trajectory radius in tight turn.
undercamber.	Concave lower airfoil surface.
under-carriage.	British term for landing gear.
USAAF.	United States Army Air Force.
Vickers FB5 gun bus.	Early British two-seater fighter; engine disliked.
Vickers gun.	Belt-fed machine gun suited for stationary use in aircraft.
Victoria Cross.	Prized British award for heroism.
wing loading.	Weight burden borne by each square foot of wing area.
yaw.	Angular offset of aircraft nose with respect to flight path, in a left-right sense.
Zero.	Japanese World War II fighter of extraordinary maneuverability.

Notes

Introduction

1. Presentation by W. S. Churchill to cabinet October 21, 1917. See Blunt, *Use of Air Power*, 165–69.
2. Ibid.
3. Hoeppner, *Deutschlands krieg in der luft*, translated as *Germany's War in the Air*, 73.
4. Ibid., 137.
5. Richthofen, *Red Air Fighter*, 73.

Chapter 1

1. PRO file #AIR 1/2150/209/3/211.
2. Ibid.
3. His emphasis. PRO file #AIR 1/1214/204/5/2631.
4. *Flight*, March 9, 1912, 222.
5. *The Aeroplane*, December 7, 1911, 222.
6. Henderson, *Art of Reconnaissance*.
7. O'Gorman, *Note Relative to Gyroscopic Couples in Aircraft*, Gt. Brit. Tech. Rept. Adv. Comm. Aero. Repts. & Memo. #81, December 1912, 196–98.
8. PRO file #AIR 1/731/176/5/102.
9. PRO file #AIR 2/4/87/504.
10. A. Mallock, *Most Dangerous Height for Aircraft Attacked from the Ground*, Gt. Brit. Tech. Rept. Adv. Comm. Aero. Repts. & Memo. #621, July 1918, 1–4.
11. PRO file #AIR 2/4/87/504.
12. Ibid.
13. Ibid.
14. Target area: 12 sq. ft. @ 400 yds.; 48 sq. ft. @ 600 yds. See Busk, *Handbook for Hythe*, 166–68.
15. PRO file #AIR 2/4/87/504.
16. *Flight*, December 7, 1912, 1127–28.
17. Ibid.
18. Chinn, *Machine Gun*, vol. 1, 278–83.
19. *Flight*, December 6, 1913, 1333.
20. In Auden and Kronenberger, *Viking Book of Aphorisms*, 102.
21. *The Aero*, April 1913, 99–104.

22. Ibid.

23. *The Aero*, April 1913, 99–104.

24. *Flight*, May 25, 1912, 467.

25. PRO file #AIR 1/811/204/4/1235.

26. PRO file #AVIA 6/1359.

27. Ibid.

28. Abstract, *Tech. Report, 1911–12*. London: Gt. Brit. Tech. Rept. Adv. Comm. Aero, 21.

29. Resulting aircraft: BS1. See *Tech. Report, 1912–13*. London: Gt. Brit. Tech. Rept. Adv. Comm. Aero, 265–68.

30. Resulting aircraft: BE2c. Ibid.

Chapter 2

1. W. Arthur Barr, *The Aeroplane*, September 11, 1913, 297; Lanchester, *Aircraft in Warfare*, 62.

2. Barr, *The Aeroplane*, September 11, 1913, 297.

3. *L'Aerophile*, August 15, 1915, 171–73.

4. Richthofen, *Red Air Fighter*, 101n.

5. Lanchester, *Aircraft in Warfare*, 62.

6. Coppens, *Days on the Wing*, 209, 210, 217, 254.

7. PRO file #AIR 1/2150/209/3/213.

8. Coppens, *Days on the Wing*, 254.

9. PRO file #AIR 1/2103/207/31.

10. PRO file #AIR 1/821/204/5/6.

11. Insall, *Observer*, 60. True for the Vickers as well.

12. Whitehouse, *Fledgling*, 131.

13. PRO file #AVIA 8/6.

14. PRO file #AIR 2/53/AB245/4155.

15. RAFM file #MFC 76/1 Brancker to Trenchard July 28, 1916.

16. PRO file #AIR 1/821/204/5/6.

17. Major Hopkinson, PRO file #AIR 2/51/AB275/2355.

18. Orfordness final report. *Notes on the Work of Orfordness Armament Experimental Station in Connection with Sights and Tactics in Aerial Gunnery.* PRO file #AIR 1/2427/305/29/942. A summing up after the war—sweeping, yet careful—our single most important source.

19. Orfordness final report. PRO file #AIR 1/2427/305/29/942.

20. Prisoner report. PRO file #AIR 1/2141/209/1/50.

21. Insall, *Observer*, 127.

22. Lambert, *Combat Report*, 123.

23. Fry, *Air of Battle*, 92.

24. PRO file #AIR 1/459/15/312/89.

25. Mortane, *Au peril de l'air*, 109.

26. Ordnance Chief, ed. *Catalog of Standard Ordnance Items*, 195.

27. Mortane, *Au peril de l'air*, 112.

28. Jullian, *La grande bataille dans les airs*, 285.

29. Sykes, *French War Birds*, 148

30. Core subject, Chambe, *Au temps des carabines*.

Chapter 3

1. *Flight*, April 25, 1918, 445.

2. *Aeronautics*, November 13, 1918, 449–51.

3. Sutherland, *Reserve Officer's Handbook*, 23.

4. The drop (in feet) equals sixteen times the bullet flight time (in seconds) squared.

5. Orfordness final report. PRO file #Air 1/2427/305/29/942, p. 20.

6. Ibid., 10.

7. Calculation: 100 MPH (or 147 ft./sec.) times 0.1 sec. = 14.7 ft., or roughly 15 ft.

8. *Aeronautics,* November 13, 1918, 449–551.

9. Orfordness final report. PRO file #AIR 1/2427/305/29/942, p. 11.

10. Ibid., p. 7–8.

11. Ibid.

12. PRO file #AIR 1/920/204/5/885.

13. Orfordness final report. PRO file #AIR 1/2427/305/29/942, pp. 7–8.

14. Ralph Sorely, wall poster, Science Museum, London.

15. Lambert, *Combat Report,* 91.

16. PRO file #AIR 1/528/16/12/65.

17. PRO file #AIR 1/1188/204/5/2595, May 22, 1917.

18. Henderson, in PRO file #AIR 1/528/16/12/65.

19. Ibid., Aug. 27, 1915.

20. Bishop, *Winged Peace,* 46.

21. Ibid.

22. Maj. L. Hawker (October 1916) believed "the noise of the gun" itself useful to signal awareness. Tracers, seen over a much greater distance, made for a stronger signal. PRO file #AIR 1/920/204/5/885.

23. Orfordness final report. PRO file #AIR 1/2427/305/29/942, p. 8.

Chapter 4

1. Orfordness final report, p. 9.

2. Mervyn O'Gorman, *Lateral Stability,* Gt. Brit. Tech. Rept. Adv. Comm. Aero. R & M #133, London, HMSO, April, 1914, figures 3 and 4.

3. Orfordness final report, p. 34.

4. Ibid., p. 29.

5. Churchill, *How to Shoot,* 89.

6. Murtz, ed., *Guns Illustrated, 1995,* 31.

7. Chambe, *Au temps des carabines,* 19, 57.

8. Wall poster, RAF Museum, Hendon, London.

9. Chambe, *Au temps des carabines,* 56.

10. Ibid., 57.

11. Morane-Saulnier, *Aeroplanes Morane-Saulnier 1914;* exchange rate, 1 Franc = 18.3 cents, New York Times, *The European War,* 477.

12. Moris usually flew the tail first version of the Shorthorn, called the Longhorn.

13. Chambe, *Au temps des carabines,* 64–65.

14. Villard, *Blue Ribbon of the Air,* 181–85, 242–43.

15. Chambe, *Au temps des carabines,* 65.

16. Jones and Rayleigh, *War in the Air,* vol. 5, 469.

17. Fry, *Air of Battle,* 41.

18. *Aeronautics,* January 1912, 19.

19. PRO file #AIR 1/748/204/3/48.

20. Ibid.

21. For E-III gun sights, see PRO files #AIR 1/910/204/5/826 and AIR 1/1061/204/5/1579, and Brannon, *Fokker Eindecker in Action,* 13, 21.

22. Brannon, *Fokker Eindecker in Action,* 13, 21.

23. Macmillan, *Sefton Brancker,* 97.

24. Orfordness final report, p. 22.

25. Armament School, Uxbridge. PRO file #AIR 1/724/75/11.

26. Buchholtz, *Der flieger Thom,* 113.

Chapter 5

1. Aldis description from PRO file #AIR 1/650/16/15/364.

2. Orfordness final report. PRO file #AIR 1/2427/305/29/942, p. 23.

3. Kilduff, trans. and ed. *Germany's Last Knight of the Air,* 66.

4. RFC Intelligence September–October 1917. PRO file #AIR 1/1188/204/5/2595.

5. Orfordness final report. PRO file #AIR 1/2427/305/29/942, 23.

6. Ibid.

7. PRO file #AIR 1/2427/305/29/942.

8. Orfordness final report. PRO file #AIR 1/2427/305/29/942, pp. 19, 23.

9. PRO file #AIR 2/51/AB275/2355.

10. Ibid.

11. Orfordness final report, p. 10.

12. PRO file #AIR 1/920/204/5/885.

13. Orfordness final report, p. 9.

14. Ibid., p. 18.

15. Experience of Lt. W. B. Farrington. PRO file #AIR 1/2386/228/11/6.

16. Orfordness final report, p. 30.

17. Ibid.

18. Rochford, *I Chose the Sky,* 134.

19. Ibid., 133.

20. Taylor, *The Sky Beyond,* 6; Vincent, *Flying Fever,* 16.

21. *Flight,* February 1, 1917, 107.

22. Statement Maj. Gen. Frederick C. Sykes, January 1919. PRO file #AIR 1/725/115/2.

23. Jackson, *Fighter Pilots of World War I,* 101.

24. Jones and Raleigh, *War in the Air,* vol. 5, 469.

25. Ibid., 426.

26. Macmillan, *Sefton Brancker,* 121. Later (April 1917) increased to 17.5 hours solo.

27. Thompson, *Lions Led by Donkeys.* A bitterly critical review of World War I leadership.

28. *The Aeroplane,* Aeronautical Engineering Supplement, January 9, 1918.

29. Capt. J. B. McCudden article in PRO file #AIR 1/920/204/5/885.

30. Survey of Squadrons No. 1, 29, 32, and 60. PRO file #AIR 1/204/5/885.

31. Survey of Martlesham Heath veteran test pilots. PRO file #AIR 1/204/5/885.

Chapter 6

1. Richthofen, *Red Air Fighter,* 116.

2. Johnstone, ed., *Naval Eight,* 195–96.

3. Orfordness final report, p. 16.

4. A. Fage and H. E. Collins, *An Investigation of the Mutual Interference of Airscrews and Bodies of the Pusher Type,* Gt. Brit. Tech. Rept. Adv. Comm. Aero. R & M #305, London, HMSO, January 1917, 325.

5. PRO file #AIR 1/160/15/123/2.

6. PRO file #AIR 1/920/204/5/885.

7. Morane-Saulnier, *Aeroplanes Morane-Saulnier,* 19.

8. Herman Glauert, *The Longitudinal Control of an Aeroplane,* Gt. Brit. Tech. Rept. Adv. Comm. Aero. R & M #592, London, HMSO, 1918, 5.

9. PRO file #AIR 1/686/21/13/2248 and PRO file #AIR 1/404/15/231/45.

10. Ibid.

11. PRO file #AIR 1/725/97/4.

12. RAFM file #76/1 letter Trenchard to Brancker, August 15, 1916.

13. RAFM file #76/1 letter Brancker to Trenchard, April 8, 1916.

14. RAFM file #76/1 letters from Trenchard to Brancker, July 1 and 13, 1916 and February 12, 1917. Also letter from Brancker to Trenchard, May 22, 1916.

15. De Havilland, *Sky Fever,* 147.

16. RAFM file #76/1 letter Trenchard to Brancker, February 12, 1917; FE8—Royal Aircraft Factory pusher fighter, rather like the DH2. See glossary.

17. Bridgeman, *Clouds Remember,* 47–52.

18. Cole, *McCudden,* 99–100.

19. Bennett, *Three Wings for the Red Baron,* chap. 6.

20. Ibid.

21. Penrose, *Great War and the Armistice,* 178–79.

22. Squadron Leader F. Maynard in PRO file #AIR 1/2388/228/11/34.

23. Penrose, *Great War and the Armistice,* 127.

24. Data from PRO file #AIR 1/1192/205/5/2599 and PRO file #AIR 1/2094/207/12/8 and PRO file #AIR 1/1/4/26/6.

25. Weyl, *Fokker: The Creative Years,* 282.

26. Gray and Thetford, *German Aircraft of the First World War,* 109.

27. PRO file #AIR 1/686/21/12/2248.

28. A. Fage and H. E. Collins, *Windage Experiments with a Model of the Rotary Engine,* Gt. Brit. Tech. Rept. Adv. Comm. Aero. R & M #448, London, HMSO, May 1918.

29. H. Kann, *Airplanes in Horizontal Curvilinear Flight* (Berlin: Technische Berichte, vol. 3, 1918, 260–67). Translated as NACA Tech. Rept. #174 (Washington, D.C., GPO).

30. Ibid.

31. Angle of attack differs slightly from incidence. Usually the difference is small, and for the sake of simplicity, we will assume the two to be identical.

32. Stewart, *Words and Music for a Mechanical Man,* 128.

33. PRO file #AIR 1/1/4/26/6.

34. McCudden, *Flying Fury: Five Years in the RFC,* 189–90.

35. Rochford, *I Chose the Sky,* 95.

36. Kilduff, *Germany's Last Knight of the Air,* 36.

37. Capt. Elliot W. Springs (16 victories) agreed, assessing the "new brand" D7 as superior to both the SE5a and Camel. See his *War Birds,* 220–22, 266, 273.

38. Jones and Rayleigh, *War in the Air,* vol. 6, 445.

39. Weyl, *Fokker: The Creative Years,* 310.

40. Bennett, *Three Wings for the Red Baron,* chap. 7.

41. Jones, *Tiger Squadron,* 74.

42. Lambert, *Combat Report,* 82. Less enthusiastic was ace Lt. Cecil Lewis, who believed late model Halberstadt and Pfalz fighters superior to the SE5. See his *All My Yesterdays,* 26.

43. French Intelligence gave the total as 338. See PRO file #AIR 1/686/21/13/2248.

44. PRO file #AVIA 6/1169 dated February 1917.

45. Ibid.

46. Warner, *Airplane Design: Aerodynamics,* chap. 6.

47. PRO file #AVIA 6/1208.

48. Ibid.

49. Springs, *War Birds*, 273.

Chapter 7

1. *The Aeroplane*, Aeronautical Engineering Supplement, January 16, 1918, 328; Triplex Safety Glass. *The Aeroplane*, February 1918, unpaginated advertisement.

2. F/Cdr. C. Draper, pilot of Pup #9906, February 1917. PRO file #AIR 1/115/15/39/51 and PRO file #AIR 1/648/17/122/397.

3. On stagger aerodynamics see Warner, *Airplane Design: Aerodynamics*, 115–24.

4. James M. Bruce, *British Aeroplanes, 1914–1918*, 182–86.

5. PRO file #AIR 1/1192/205/5/2599/ parts 1, 2, 3.

6. *Aeroplane Monthly*, August 2001, 22–24.

7. PRO file #AVIA 6/1159.

8. *The Aeroplane*, April 18, 1917, 958–59.

Chapter 8

1. Cooksley, *Air V.C.'s*, 23.

2. Cole *Royal Flying Corps Communiqués*, 17.

3. Cooksley, *Air V.C.'s*, 29.

4. Hip length boots of sheepskin, designed for warmth. The "double" was never liked. Heavy and offering high drag, it was difficult to load. Rumors had it subject to many more jams, when compared to the standard drum. For Hawker inventions, see Hawker, *Hawker V.C.*, 149–51, 173.

5. Ibid., 169.

6. Ibid., 172.

7. Climb values obtained through differentiation of data. Bruce, *British Aeroplanes, 1914–1918*, 163–64 and *Flugsport*, October 1919, 702.

8. Bruce, *British Aeroplanes, 1914–1918*, 163.

9. PRO file #AIR 1/1000/204/5/1252.

10. Spiraling and circling tactics as given by PRO file #AVIA 6/2366.

11. Plot: original; data calculated from expression given by Warner, *Airplane Design: Aerodynamics*, 510, as applied to Allied aircraft specifications from NASM archives, and German aircraft specifications from *Flugsport*, October 1919, 702 and November 1919, 829.

12. Our original calculations, from data in F. H. Norton and H. Allen, "Control in Circling Flight," NACA Tech. Rept. #112, Washington D.C.: USGPO, 1921.

13. Our original calculations, from data in Heinrich Kann, "Airplanes in Horizontal Curvilinear Flight," FlugM. Tech. Ber., Berlin, 1918, vol. 3, 260–67.

14. Breakaway concepts from PRO file #AIR 1/1625/204/89/8.

15. PRO file #AIR 1/920/204/5/885.

16. Richthofen, *Red Air Fighter*, 83–85, gave his initial altitude as 10,000 feet, with Hawker launching his own attack from a still greater altitude. We doubt it; DH2 performance at those altitudes was too feeble to support combat. Instead, we accept a more believable initial altitude of 8,000 feet, offered by Nowarra and Brown's *Von Richthofen and the Flying Circus*, 35.

17. Official instruction as of September 1916. PRO file #AIR 1/1625/204/89/8.

18. Richthofen, *Red Air Fighter*, 84.

19. Ibid., 85.

20. Hawker, *Hawker V.C.*, 233–34.

21. Malfunctions taken from data in Ibid., 140–41.

22. Richthofen, *Red Air Fighter*, 83.

23. Titler, *The Day the Red Baron Died;* Carisella and Ryan, *Who Killed the Red Baron?;* Franks and Bennett, *The Red Baron's Last Flight: A Mystery Investigated.*

24. Bennett, *Three Wings,* chap. 1.

25. Bishop, *Winged Peace,* 52–53; 26. Springs, *War Birds,* 167; 27; Jones, *An Air Fighter's Scrapbook,* 54, respectively.

26. Orange, *Sir Keith Park,* 28.

27. Titler's *The Day the Red Baron Died,* 201, 215, strongly disagreed, alleging the existence of many additional bullets and bullet wounds. It was Titler's view that these somehow managed to escape detection by two medical teams charged with Richthofen's autopsy. Titler presented no evidence for his curious beliefs and we find his case unacceptable.

28. Richthofen's engine, on display, may be examined at the Imperial War Museum, London, United Kingdom.

29. Bishop, *Winged Peace,* 52.

30. Orfordness final report. PRO file #1/2427/305/29/942, p. 33.

31. A. Mallock, *Most Dangerous Height for Aircraft Attacked from the Ground,* Gt. Brit. Tech. Rept. Adv. Comm. Aero. R & M #621, London, HMSO, July 1918.

32. The odds are given by 0.5 to the 80th power, or approximately = 8.3 with the decimal point 25 places to the left. For a good popular description of this classic statistics problem see Paulos, *Mathematician Reads the Newspaper,* 181–83.

33. Ibid. The odds are given by 0.5 to the 10th power.

34. Ibid. The odds are given by 0.5 to the 5th power.

Chapter 9

1. The number of workers, each capable of producing N achievements, is proportional to $1/N^2$. See Price, *Little Science, Big Science,* 42–45.

2. The concept is well known. If $y = x^n$, then $\log y = n \log x$, or $\log y/\log x = n$. In words, the slope of a log-log plot equals the exponent n. As a check, a protractor gives the slope of the Lotka's Law plot as 63 degrees. Looking up the tangent of 63 degrees yields 2.0 or, $y = x^2$.

3. Bucek, ed., *Baseball Encyclopedia,* 1781–1800.

4. German victories are taken from ZFM, December 1918, Appendix 17–18·and www.crossandcockade.com.

5. Bowyer, *Albert Ball, V.C.,* 64–68.

6. Richthofen, *Red Air Fighter,* 135.

7. British victories are taken from Shores et al., *Above the Trenches* and www.crossand cockade.com.

8. Revell, *Brief Glory,* 127.

9. Bowyer, *Albert Ball, V.C.,* 127.

10. Ishoven, *Fall of an Eagle,* 67.

11. Pershing, *My Experiences in the World War,* vol. 2, 162.

12. Richthofen, *Red Air Fighter,* 167–75.

13. Kilduff, *Richthofen: Beyond the Legend of the Red Baron,* 107–11.

14. Intelligence from captured pilot (November 1917). PRO file #AIR 1/2251/209/54/25.

15. Nowarra and Brown, *Von Richthofen and the Flying Circus,* 90; accounts of the Brest-Litovsk negotiations assigned no role to Richthofen. Our guess: he was a trophy delegate whose function was to impress the Bolsheviks. See Wheeler-Bennett, *Brest-Litovsk.*

16. Shores, et al., *Above the Trenches,* 76.

17. Ibid., 114–15.

18. Cole, *McCudden, V.C.,* 158.

19. Cunningham, *Mac's Memoirs*, 26.

20. Air Ministry Publication #3139, *Psychological Disorders in Flying Personnel of the Royal Air Force*, 157–58.

21. Colonel Repington was known as a behind-the-scenes negotiator and sounding board. His memoirs remain lively; Repington, *First World War*, 2 vols.; *The Aeroplane*, June 19, 1918, 2242.

22. *The Aeroplane*, June 19, 1918, 2242.

23. PRO file #AIR 1/920/204/5/885.

24. Ibid.

25. Boyle, *Trenchard*, 168–71.

26. *Air Training Corps Gazette*, July 1943, 12 and *Flight*, October 18, 1917, 1070.

27. PRO file #AIR 1/920/204/5/885.

28. E-III ferry pilot captured April 1916. Plane liked by noncommissioned pilot because "it meant taking no observer and he disliked playing second fiddle." PRO file #AIR 1/2141/209/1/50.

Bibliography

Official Documentation (Archives) and Official Technical Serial Publications
Australian War Memorial Photograph Database, Canberra, Australia.
Flugmeisterei Technische Berichte (given as FlugM. Tech. Ber.).
Great Britain Technical Report Advisory Committee for Aeronautics Report and Memoranda
    (given as Gt. Brit. Tech. Rept. Adv. Comm. Aero. R & M #).
IWM file #, Imperial War Museum, Lambeth Road, London, United Kingdom.
National Advisory Committee for Aeronautics Technical Report # (given as NACA Tech.
    Rept. #).
National Air and Space Museum (given as NASM).
PRO file #, Public Record Office, Kew, London, United Kingdom.
RAFM file #, Royal Air Force Museum, Hendon, London, United Kingdom.

Books
Air Ministry Publication #3139. *Psychological Disorders in Flying Personnel of the Royal Air
    Force.* London: HMSO, 1947.
Auden, W. H., and Louis Kronenberger. *Viking Book of Aphorisms.* New York: Viking, 1962.
Baer, E. H., ed. *Der Volkerkrieg.* Vols. 2 and 14. Stuttgart, Germany: Hoffmann, 1914 and
    1917.
Bennett, Leon. *Three Wings for the Red Baron.* Shippensburg, Pa.: White Mane, 2000.
Bishop, William A. *Winged Peace.* New York: Viking, 1944.
———. *Winged Warfare.* New York: Hodder and Stoughton, 1918.
Blunt, V. E. R. *The Use of Air Power.* London: Thorsens, 1942.
Bowan, Ezra. *Knights of the Air.* Alexandria, Va.: Time-Life, 1980.
Bowyer, Chaz. *Albert Ball, V.C.* London: William Kimber, 1977.
Boyle, Andrew. *Trenchard.* London: Collins, 1962.
Brannon, Edgar D. *Fokker Eindecker in Action.* Carrolton, Tex.: Squadron/Signal, 1996.
Bridgeman, Leonard. *The Clouds Remember.* London: Gale and Polden, n.d.
Bruce, J. M. *British Aeroplanes, 1914–1918.* London: Putnam, 1969.
Bucek, J., ed. *The Baseball Encyclopedia.* 10th ed. New York: Macmillan, 1996.
Buchholtz, Hansgeorg. *Der flieger Thom.* Konigsberg, Germany: Grafe and Unzer, 1937.
Burda, Franz. *Fuenfzig Jahre Motorflug.* Offenburg, Germany: printed by Burda, 1953.
Busk, Hans. *Handbook for Hythe.* London: Routledge, Warne and Routledge, 1860; reprint,
    Richmond, United Kingdom: Richmond Publishing, 1971.

Carisella, P. J., and J.W. Ryan. *Who Killed the Red Baron?* Wakefield, Mass.: Daedalus, 1969.

Chambe, Rene. *Au temps des carabines.* Paris: Flammarion, 1955.

Chinn, George M. *The Machine Gun.* 3 vols. Washington, D.C.: Navy Department, GPO, 1951.

Christienne, Charles, and Pierre Lissarrague. *French Military Aviation.* Washington D.C.: Smithsonian Institution Press, 1986.

Churchill, Robert. *How to Shoot.* London: Geoffrey Bles, 1925.

Cole, Christopher. *McCudden, V.C.* London: William Kimber, 1967.

———. *Royal Flying Corps Communiqués, 1915–1916.* London: William Kimber, 1969.

Cooke, James J. *The U.S. Air Service in the Great War.* Westport, Conn.: Praeger, 1996.

Cooksley, Peter G. *The Air V.C.'s.* Gloucestershire, United Kingdom: Sutton, 1996; reprint, London: Wrens Park, 1999.

Coppens, Willi. *Days on the Wing.* London: Hamilton, 1934.

Cunningham, G. H. *Mac's Memoirs.* Wellington, New Zealand, 1937.

De Havilland, Geoffrey. *Sky Fever.* London: Hamish Hamilton, 1961.

Dudgeon, J. M. *Mick: The Story of Maj. Edward Mannock.* London: Robert Hale, 1981.

Fonck, Rene. *Ace of Aces.* New York: Doubleday, 1967.

Franks, Norman, and Alan Bennett. *The Red Baron's Last Flight: A Mystery Investigated.* Ontario: Vanwell, 1997.

Fry, William. *Air of Battle.* London: William Kimber, 1974.

Gray, Peter, and Owen Thetford. *German Aircraft of the First World War.* London: Putnam, 1962.

Hall, Norman S. *The Balloon Buster.* New York: Doubleday, Doran, 1928.

Hawker, Tyrrel M. *Hawker, V.C.* London: Mitre Press, 1965.

Henderson, David. *The Art of Reconnaissance,* 3rd edition. London: Murray, 1914.

Herlin, Hans. *Udet: A Man's Life.* London: Macdonald, 1960.

Hoeppner, Ernst von. *Deutschlands krieg in der luft.* Leipzig, K. F. Koehler, 1921. Translated as *Germany's War in the Air.* Nashville: Battery Press, 1994.

Insall, Algernon J. *Observer.* London: William Kimber, 1970.

Ishoven, Armand van. *Ernst Udet.* Berlin: Neff, 1977.

———. *The Fall of an Eagle.* London: William Kimber, 1979.

Jackson, Robert. *Fighter Pilots of World War I.* New York: St. Martin's Press, 1972.

Johnstone, E. G., ed. *Naval Eight.* London: Arms and Armour, 1972.

Jones, H. A. *The War in the Air,* 7 vols. Oxford: Clarendon, 1937.

Jones, Henry, and Walter Rayleigh. *War in the Air.* 6 vols., appendix, and atlas. London: Oxford, 1922–37.

Jones, Ira. *An Air Fighter's Scrapbook.* London: Nicholson and Watson, 1938; reprint, London: Greenhill, 1990.

———. *King of Air Fighters.* London: Nicholson and Watson, 1934.

———. *Tiger Squadron.* London: W. H. Allen, 1954; reprint, London: Award Books, 1966.

Joubert, Philip Sir. *The Third Service.* London: Thames and Hudson, 1955.

Jullian, Marcel. *La grande bataille dans les airs.* Paris: Presses de la Cite, 1967.

Kilduff, Peter. *Richthofen: Beyond the Legend of the Red Baron.* London: Arms and Armour, 1995.

Kilduff, Peter, trans. and ed. *Germany's Last Knight of the Air.* London: William Kimber, 1979.

Lambert, William C. *Combat Report.* London: William Kimber, 1973; reprint, London: Corgi, 1975.

Lanchester, Frederick W. *Aircraft in Warfare.* London: Constable, 1916.

Lewis, Cecil. *Sagittarius Rising.* London: Davies, 1936; reprint, London: Warner, 1994.

————. *All My Yesterdays*. Dorset, United Kingdom: Element Books, 1993.

Macmillan, Norman. *Sefton Brancker*. London: Heinemann, 1935.

————. *Great Aircraft*. New York: St. Martin's Press, 1960.

Marck, Bernard. *Le dernier vol de Guynemer*. Paris: Acropole, 1991.

Maurer, Maurer, ed., *The U.S. Air Service in World War I*. 4 vols. Washington D.C.: GPO, 1978.

McCudden, James. *Flying Fury: Five Years in the RFC*. London: Aviation Book Club, 1930; reprint, London: Greenhill, 1987.

Morane-Saulnier. *Aeroplanes Morane-Saulnier 1914*. Commercial catalog, privately printed, Paris, 1914. Available Library of Congress, Washington, D.C.

Mortane, Jacques. *Au peril de l'air*. Paris: Editions Baudiniere, 1936.

Murtz, H. A., ed. *Guns Illustrated, 1995*. Northbrook, Ill.: DBI Books, 1995.

New York Times. *The European War*, vol. 7. New York: New York Times, 1917.

Nowarra, H., and K. Brown. *Von Richthofen and the Flying Circus*. London: Letchworth, 1964.

Orange, Vincent. *Sir Keith Park*. London: Methuen, 1984.

Ordnance Chief, ed. *Catalog of Standard Ordnance Items*. Vol. 2. Washington, D.C.: GPO, 1944.

Paulos, John Allen. *A Mathematician Reads the Newspaper*. New York: Anchor, 1995.

Penrose, Harold. *The Great War and the Armistice*. New York: Funk and Wagnall's, 1969.

Perkins, C. D., and Robert E. Hage. *Airplane Performance Stability and Control*. New York: Wiley, 1949.

Pershing, John J. *My Experiences in the World War*. 2 vols. New York: Stokes, 1931.

Price, Derek J. *Little Science, Big Science*. New York: Columbia University Press, 1963.

Pugachev, V. S. *Teoria Vozdushnoi Strel'by*. Moscow, 1940.

Ralph, Wayne. *Barker, V.C.* Toronto: Doubleday Canada, 1997.

Repington, C. A. C. *The First World War*. 2 vols. London: Constable, 1920.

Revell, Alex. *Brief Glory*. London: William Kimber, 1984.

Richthofen, Manfred von. *The Red Air Fighter*. London: Aeroplane and General Publishing, 1918; reprint, Bath: Chivers, 1967; reprint, London: Greenhill, 1990.

Rickenbacker, Edward V. *Fighting the Flying Circus*. New York: Stokes, 1919.

————. *Rickenbacker*. Englewood Cliffs, N.J.: Prentice-Hall, 1967.

Rochford, Leonard H. *I Chose the Sky*. London: William Kimber, 1977.

Rogers, Bogart. *A Yankee Ace in the RAF*. Lawrence: University Press of Kansas, 1996.

Scott, A. J. L. *Sixty Squadron, RAF*. London: Heinemann, 1920; reprint, London: Greenhill, 1990.

Shores, Christopher, et al. *Above the Trenches*. London: Grub Street, 1990.

Springs, Elliot W. *War Birds*. New York: Grosset and Dunlap, 1926.

Stewart, Oliver. *Words and Music for a Mechanical Man*. London: William Kimber, 1967.

Sutherland, S. J. *The Reserve Officer's Handbook*. Boston: Houghton Mifflin, 1917.

Sykes, Claud W. *French War Birds*. London: Hamilton, 1937; reprint, London, Greenhill, 1987.

Tanner, John, ed., *Fighting in the Air*. RAF Museum Series, vol. 7. London: Arms and Armour, 1978.

Taylor, Gordon. *The Sky Beyond*. Boston: Houghton Mifflin, 1963; reprint, New York: Ballantine, 1970.

Thompson, Peter Anthony. *Lions Led by Donkeys*. London: Laurie, 1927.

Titler, Dale M. *The Day the Red Baron Died*. New York: Ballantine, 1970.

Udet, Ernst. *Ace of the Iron Cross*. New York: Arco, 1970.

————. *Hals und Beinbruch*. Berlin: Wilhelm Kolf, 1928.

Vaughan, David K., ed. *An American Pilot in the Skies of France*. Dayton, Ohio: Wright State University Press, 1992.

Villard, Henry S. *Blue Ribbon of the Air*. Washington D.C: Smithsonian Books, 1987.

Vincent, S. F. *Flying Fever*. London: Jarrolds, 1972.

Warner, Edward. *Airplane Design: Aerodynamics*. New York: McGraw-Hill, 1927.

Weyl, A. R. *Fokker: The Creative Years*. London: Putnam, 1965.

Wheeler-Bennett, John W. *Brest-Litovsk*. New York: Norton, 1971.

Whitehouse, Arch. *The Fledgling*. New York: Duell, Sloan and Pierce, 1964.

Windrow, Martin C., ed. *Aircraft in Profile*. Vol. 5, chap. 7, by J. M. Bruce. New York: Doubleday, 1970.

Aero Journals

Aeronautics, United Kingdom, January 1912–November 13, 1918.

The Aero, United Kingdom, September, 1912–April 1913.

L'Aerophile, France, August 1, 1912–August 15, 1915.

The Aeroplane, United Kingdom, December 7, 1911–June 19, 1918.

Air Training Corps Gazette, United Kingdom, July 1943.

Deutsche Luftfahrer Zeitung, Germany (given as DLZ).

Flight, United Kingdom, March 9, 1912–January 28, 1919.

Flying, United States, November 1914.

Flug, Austria, July 1913–December 1916.

Flugsport, Germany, March 1917–November 1919.

Luftfahrt, Germany, April 1918.

U.S. Air Service, United States.

Zeitschrift fur Flugtecknik und Motorlieftschiffahrt Germany, (given as ZFM), December 1918.

Index

mortar (airborne), 26–28

Nonflamoid (plastic), 132
Norman vane, *see* gun sight, vane

observation (aerial), 1, 16–17
O'Gorman, Mervyn, 8–12, 15, 17–18, 113, 117

Parabellum gun, 39, 41, 104–105
Park, Maj. Keith., 159
Patrick, Maj. Cochrane, 48, 50–52
Pegoud, Alphonse, 19, 21
performance (aircraft)
  ceiling, 149–53
  climb, 107–108, 112, 119–22, 126–30, 133–35, 145–50
  maneuverability, 107–108, 121–30, 133–35, 139, 140, 145–53, 156
  speed, 107, 108, 112, 119–30, 135, 145–46
production (aircraft), 107, 109
propeller (vulnerability), 18–20, 115

RAF, 99, 108, 177–78
range (air fighting), 65–68, 72–73, 78, 86, 88, 95
Repington, Col. C.A.C. 177–78
RFC (Royal Flying Corps), 6, 8, 19, 34, 72, 83, 95, 98–99, 144, 156, 165, 177
Rhys-Davids, Lt. A.P.F., 25, 29, 172
Rice, Capt. S.R., 18
von Richthofen, Rittmeister Manfred (Red Baron)
  background, 3, 5, 45, 108, 140
  combat, 155–74, 182
  conclusion, 186
Rickenbacker, Capt. Eddie, 29
rifle, riflemen, 10–13, 159–62, 186
RNAS (Royal Naval Air Service), 28–29, 108
Rochford, Sq. Ldr. Leonard H., 95, 124
Rogers, Lt B., 29

Royal Aircraft Factory, 8, 9, 117

Salmond, Gen. J.M., 179
Scarff (mount), 37
shotgun, 26, 69
Sigrist, Fred, 117
Sopwith
  Aircraft Co., 139
  Camel, *see* British aircraft types
  Pup, *see* British aircraft types
Sopwith, Tom, 115
Sorely, Ralph, 54
Spandau machine gun, 30, 77
Springs, Capt. Elliot, 129, 159
Stewart, Lt. Oliver, 124
stoppage (machine gun) 27–34, 40
Sykes, Capt. Frederick H., 16

Thom, Ltn. Karl, 78
Tiverton, Lt.,41
tracers, 5, 47, 52–61, 184
Trenchard, Gen. Hugo M., 35, 98, 112–113, 179

Udet, Ltn. Ernst, 168–69, 173, 182

Vergnette, Capt. de, 70–72
Vickers gun
  conclusion, 184
  history, 11, 113–15, 117, 178
  operation (jams), 27–35, 38–40, 42–46, 67, 81, 103, 161
Victoria Cross, 142
victories, 165, 169–82, 186
vision, 127–39

Whitehouse, Sgt. Arch, 34

yaw, 65–66, 72, 90

Zeppelin, 1, 4, 8